MEMOIR OF MANHATTAN

MEMOIR OF MANHATTAN

The Way We Were

Diane Brenda Bryan

This book was printed in the United States of America.
Xlibris: A STRATEGIC PARTNER OF RANDOM HOUSE VENTURES

To order additional copies of this book, contact:
Xlibris Corporation
1-888-795-4274
www.Xlibris.com
Orders@Xlibris.com
37539

CONTENTS

DEDICATED WITH LOVE
TO
MOMMA AND MORRIS

Who taught me what it means to be a "mensch"

And, as always, with love to my children: Jeffrey, Ellen and Jonathan, who are so much a part of these treasured memories.

ACKNOWLEDGMENTS

With thanks to my colleagues: Mark Jacoby (in memoriam), David Shapiro, and Donald Silverman for their constructive suggestions, support and friendship.

"Old streets and familiar places haunt me, invading my thoughts.
In sepia tones, shadowy figures pass along dim streets and I move in
parallel fashion, dreamlike. Gradually, I begin to move more definitively,
more positively in that Yesterday, growing up in Manhattan.

Ah, if only I could once more walk on the sidewalks of New York."

Diane Brenda Bryan

THE AUTHOR IN AN EARLY PHOTO SHOOT ON THIRD STREET

CHAPTER 1

EAST SIDE, WEST SIDE

All around the town
Tots play ring-a-rosy
London Bridge is falling down;
Boys and girls together
Me and Mamie O'Rourke,
We trip the light fantastic
On the sidewalks of New York.

That was the song we sang a long time ago. I still remember it. Nostalgia.

Today, in the words of that famous tunesmith Billy Joel, old Manhattanites reflect, "I'm in a New York state of mind." I always was; always will be. My hometown.

New York is the most fabulous city in the world—a place where dreams sometimes come true, but never die. Its inhabitants are streetwise, courageous and ambitious. Survivors handle the heat; others fall by the wayside. At least, that's how I remember it.

During the post-Depression era, on the East Side (now the East Village), we grew up tough. There weren't too many automobiles around then; we played our games in the streets and backyards: ring-a-levio, potsy, stick ball, jump rope, hide and go seek—all innocent camaraderie and always clean fun.

The mere mention of New York City evokes a sense of excitement, an aura of expectation. NEW YORK! . . . the City to which strong entrepreneurial masses came pouring out of cargo holds onto Ellis Island, yearning for freedom.

Considering early American cities, I marvel that New York is the oldest of these historic places—more so than Philadelphia or Boston or Williamsburg. Why was New York named for the Duke of York who never set foot in the City?

I'm not writing this to dwell on ancient history. This is my story—old enough—of my childhood and youth, as I lived it in the first half of the 20th Century. This is a memoir of Manhattan as I remember it way back when.

Come along, enjoy, reminisce and, perhaps, share a memory or two.

CHAPTER 2

PROLOGUE TO A LIFE

Time: Winter, 8 January 1923
Place: 32 East 3rd Street, Manhattan

E sther Bryan, determined and resolute, stood in the far corner of the room. It was in the early hours before the dawn of January 8th, 1923. Outside, a blizzard raged and the wild wind whirled the snow around the front of the old brownstone and tore across the City streets and alleyways. Inside, a hush descended over all as a miracle unfolded.

The doctor, feverishly summoned, had made his way down the dark, hazardous streets through high drifts of snow as he was badgered by the forceful wind. The door was opened even before he knocked and he was hurried up the stairs to a bedchamber wherein awaited his task. The young girl in the four-poster bed was almost lost in the folds of the huge comforter and pillows which enveloped her. In spite of her sobbing, she blinked welcoming eyes. *At last, the doctor was here and all would be well.*

Esther reflected on what brought this circumstance about, gathered this little group of almost strangers together and was about to alter her life irrevocably. A beautiful, intelligent woman, she had braved the transition from the Old World to the New . . . the hard way. She had courage that most men would envy and a sense of self that women would not achieve until later in the century. Yet she felt a fear she had not experienced since marauding Cossacks galloped through her small town in Poland. She panicked now. *Can I do this? Can she do this? Can we both do what we had agreed to: She, to give up her baby; I, to take it as my own.*

What do I know about taking care of a baby? Old World wisdom prevailed. *I am a woman, am I not? Of course, I'll know what to do. It will come naturally.* She smiled confidently. *Incredible! This lovely, young girl bringing a new life into the world, at the same time crying, happy and sad. And, here am I, thirty-five years of age, watching the birth of a child I would soon call my own.*

Esther remembered the day Rose had knocked upon her door—her young, handsome husband, Harry, not far behind. They came to the little gate at the entranceway, saying that a family friend had recommended they visit her to discuss their dilemma. Esther scrutinized the hapless pair, suspicious of what she might hear and invited them in, immediately offering a cup of tea.

As they sipped their tea, the girl said nothing for several minutes. Finally, Rose blurted out, "Our parents are going to annul our marriage because we are so young. I can't tell them we're going to have a baby. But, we will marry someday when we are able to. Right now we are desperate and heartbroken." A flow of tears followed. Esther's suspicions were confirmed.

She had always wanted to have children but could not. Regretfully, she never attempted to rectify the problem medically. Now this sweet, young soon-to-be mother was making a proposal, stuttering, stammering, almost out of control, seeking the right words. "Could you, please . . . would you take my baby so I will know where it is and that it is in a good home. Would you do this . . . such a blessing . . . such a favor . . . to ease our pain?"

Esther held her hand, all the while holding back tears of her own, her heart filled with compassion. "Yes, yes, of course. Don't worry, dear." But, she knew it was going to be difficult to say these next words. She drew in her breath. "I will take the baby as my own, but you must be willing to give up any claim to this child. The baby must be mine completely because I won't be able to live with the pain of watching the child torn between us."

Tears welled up in Rose's eyes and she sobbed uncontrollably. Finally, she agreed to relinquish all ties "with a broken heart but for the good of my baby."

Thus, it was arranged that when her time approached, Rose would bed down in Esther's house where she would receive care and medical attention. So it came to pass, in the twilight hours of that stormy winter morning, in that old brownstone, a sleepy doctor was summoned from his warm bed to deliver one tiny, underweight three and three-quarter pound girl, who, when slapped resoundingly on the fanny, uttered a cry of protest that pierced the morning air but brought tears of joy to all present.

Curtain rise.

ENTER: Diane Brenda Bryan

CHAPTER 3

THIRD STREET

So many years have gone by, yet it's strange how sometimes in the course of a hectic day, I pause and find myself going down an empty street in my memory, the sound of my footsteps echoing in my ears. Once again, I'm the child I was, long ago, only yesterday. The hollow footsteps upon the pavement stir up memories of other sounds . . . of other people . . . of other times. In those stirrings is the story of another day.

The old cobblestones of the 19th Century still remained in some places but few vestiges remained of that earlier time. That long ago street! The old gas lit residences converted into rooming houses; the aged apartment houses (walk-ups) with their dark railroad flats and fire escapes; ancient, creaking stairways in dimly lit hallways; old, wooden gazebos in backyards where families could "picnic" when the weather was too hot to stay indoors. It was during the hot weather when sleep was almost impossible in stuffy rooms that people took to the fire escapes with their pillows and quilts, perhaps to catch a breeze which would enable them to sleep. Depending on how much room there was on the fire escape, the children were always given preference. We weren't afraid in those days.

If I close my eyes and listen carefully, I can hear the call of the iceman. Here he comes with his horse-drawn wagon filled with huge blocks of ice, to fill the ice boxes in the apartments so that food may be preserved and edible for at least a couple of days. Under each ice box was a pan into which the ice melted. If the pan wasn't emptied on time, the kitchen became a "lake". The iceman was always a welcome sight. We kids would all clamor around the truck. He knew that what we really were interested in were the chips of ice that fell when he cut the blocks into sizeable chunks. As soon as he strapped onto his back a cake of ice held in place by huge tongs, we all jumped onto the wagon and grabbed some chips to suck on. That was great fun. Imagine! Not so much fun for the poor, hardworking iceman who had to repeat his burdened journey up flights of stairs, over and over again.

There were other wagons that came into the neighborhood: the fruit and vegetable vendors who would ring a bell to herald their arrival. From the buildings would stream the women with children in hand, to see what items they could afford that day. The little ones would stand by hoping for a peach or an orange that, perhaps, the merchant might be inclined to throw to them . . . which he often did. In the post-Depression, a piece of fresh fruit was a real prize. It was fun listening to the haggling over the prices which was an important part of community activity.

One of the most thrilling visitors, to me, was the man who came around with his little pony to take pictures of Mother's pride and joy. I always wanted to sit on that pony and one day Momma said we would have a picture taken. Overjoyed, I sat on that pony like Annie Oakley, not flinching a muscle. It was such a thrill. Judging from the expression on my face, I was a most happy kid. I still have that picture. Looking at it stirs up thoughts of how sweet and simple life was then and how we found pleasure in innocent pursuits.

*   *   *

There was a little grocery just down the street, around the corner on Second Avenue. When I reached a trustworthy age, Momma sent me, early in the morning, to fill up a bottle of milk from the huge cans just outside the store. I would ladle in the milk and cover the bottle. Sometimes, I was told to buy fresh, sweet tasting rolls or a piece of delicious corn or rye bread. Selection depended on our finances. I delighted in speaking with older people, so I always managed a little conversation with the grocer before I hurried home.

Across the street, on the opposite corner, was the drugstore where we purchased all our medicinal needs and toiletries. I could even get a candy bar there and it would be "charged" to our family account—sales noted on a slip of paper. I don't recall how it happened, but one day I decided that Ex-Lax was a darned good-tasting chocolate. After requesting several packages as the day wore on, the druggist, now a little suspicious, decided to ask my mother if indeed she was sending me over to buy all that Ex-Lax.

That evening was no fun.

Next door to the druggists was a kosher delicatessen from which wafted the most delectable odors of grilled frankfurters, steaming meats, golden french fries, and the garlic pickles heaped in bowls upon the tables. There was one table at which my father and I sat ever so often, devouring some savory temptations. I always think it strange that I recall this particular memory of my adopted father, Jacob Bryan. Another vague memory is that he owned a car and often, on Sundays, we would ride out to the countryside. I loved falling asleep on the back seat. He was a handsome man and popular, particularly with the ladies, I later found out. Some faint memories linger in the dusty corners of my mind.

That street, Third Street. So different now. The camera of my memory moves and captures yet another image: a blustery time when the snows and the winds of the season were upon us: winter, when my friends and I rolled in the snow and giggled as we threw snowballs at each other. On Christmas, the children of the neighborhood were invited to visit Santa at the YMCA, which was right up the street, near Third Avenue. We stood in line, oblivious to the freezing temperatures, waiting to be admitted to that sanctum sanctorum. Finally, there HE was, Santa Claus, surrounded by a multitude of wonderful gaily wrapped, enticing gifts. We were overwhelmed. As we stepped up to this impressive icon, each of us kissed him quickly on the cheek, clutching the offered gifts to our bosoms. Rushing back out into the street, we eagerly compared our presents before joyfully racing back to the flats and basement apartments that were home.

Whether it was Christmas or Chanukah, the memory of that seasonal token of generosity always lingers as a happy one.

When I was still pretty much a little kid, I was fascinated by the group of Salvation Army singers that came to our corner, dressed in blue capes and bonnets and with tambourines in hand, to sing hymns. They were usually there when it was my nap time and I had to sneak down the stoop to stand near them. Momma never understood why I had a sudden interest in wearing a blue cape but thought I'd look cute in one, so she indulged me. When I asked for a tambourine, she mistook this to mean a budding interest in music, so I soon had a tambourine. She drew the line at the blue bonnet request. I never wore hats. That's probably where I blew it. My deception was revealed when Momma, suspicious, emerged from our ground floor apartment and caught me, tambourine in hand, trying to sing about "the blood of the lamb."

Her firm hand led me back to my bed. She advised me that my tambourine playing, from now on, would be done in the kitchen.

Such was life on Third Street where the last vestiges of the old trolley car remained on Second Avenue . . . the decrepit tracks still winding their way uptown and down, even though the trolley soon ceased to run. I recall that ancient chariot swaying as it made its way up the Avenue, and I'll never forget the feeling of adventure and excitement it evoked in my imagination as it rattled by amidst the hustle bustle on its trip to that mysterious uptown.

CHAPTER 4

SCHOOL DAYS—IN THE BEGINNING

J attended the old, brick elementary school on Third Street, between First Avenue and Avenue A, in kindergarten and grades 1 and 2. I can still picture that ancient edifice with its schoolyard, a few steps up from the sidewalk, surrounded by a huge wrought iron fence.

My mother told me I created quite a commotion at the beginning of the school year during milk and cookies time. I wanted my bottle. Never could understand why I was still on the bottle. Blame it on my youth.

How I came to attend school at the age of five is a story in itself. As far as I know (from what Momma said), the principal of the school passed our house everyday, at which time I was usually playing in the street, with my mother on guard duty. One day, he asked, "How come your little boy is not in school?"

"This is not my little boy; this is my little girl," Momma informed him. "And, besides, she is not old enough to go to school."

I guess I looked older because I was tall. She promised that she would bring me to school as soon as I was the right age. I was then four and a half; I was in school by the time I was five.

Surviving kindergarten, I progressed eventually from first to second grade . . . and that is where an obsession gripped me. Everyday just before we were dismissed for lunch, teacher would announce, "Everybody with a lunch bag, form a line at the door." This done, the children with brown bags in hand were marched down the hall to "that room". That room completely captured my imagination. Talk about visions dancing in your head. I was sure the kids with the brown bags were enjoying some privileged, special experience.

I never got to bring lunch because we lived two avenue blocks away, and every day my dad fetched me home where Momma had lunch waiting. By one o'clock, he returned me to school. Many are the times I hinted that perhaps I could bring my own little brown bag. This was received with a resounding "What!" Momma couldn't believe that I would prefer that to a freshly prepared lunch. The truth is, I think my mother didn't want me away from her for the whole day. I still remember the midday inspection: were my limbs intact; did I have a fever, maybe; did my stomach hurt . . . after which I was ready to eat, with gusto.

That room in school, however, preyed on my mind, until one day I devised a plan. I would smuggle a piece of my breakfast roll into a brown bag and secret it in my coat pocket. Surprisingly, when my plan went into action, there were no hitches. Sitting at my little desk, I tingled with excitement. "Today, I will join that special group."

What images I conjured up! That room would be bright and cheerful with little wooden tables decorated with pretty pictures, dishes flanked by shiny knives, forks and spoons; and, little cups painted with fairytale characters. The children would be merrily chatting as they ate lunch and later would sing happy songs together.

The morning dragged by. I could hardly wait. Finally, lunchtime. When the teacher made her usual announcement, I stood up confidently and joined the line. At last, no more imagining, no more dreaming, no more yearning.

We were ushered into a room and told, "Take a seat and eat your lunch quietly." Anticipation quickly turned into disappointment as I gazed about the room. Why, it was just a plain, old classroom . . . same rows of seats with small desks; same ceiling-high windows; same lights. No pretty table settings, no chit chats, no singing—just, "Eat and be quiet!"

I found a seat near the back of the room and surreptitiously opened my brown bag, desperately hoping to avoid any attention. To my dismay, the pathetic fragment of bread drew an immediate reaction from old "eagle eye". The teacher charged over to me and demanded, "Where is your lunch?"

"This is my lunch," I stammered as I held back tears. I could hear the children giggling. Thank goodness, they were quickly silenced.

I think if I hadn't confessed to my prank, my parents would have been hauled into court on charges of child neglect and abuse. After I spilled the beans, a phone call was made home. Good thing, because by now my parents were frantic and ready to call the police. They immediately rushed to the principal's office. Words of thanks tumbled from their lips. I was too embarrassed to say a word but I knew I would hear plenty later.

Spanking was not a discipline used at home until that afternoon when my father's frustration must have reached extraordinary heights. He whacked me on the backside with one resounding w-a-a-p, after which I was quick to assure them that I was truly sorry, yea, remorseful and that, hereafter, I would be most appreciative of lunch at home.

The whole unappetizing experience left quite an impression upon me. Sitting down that night was a most frangible and tender experience.

CHAPTER 5

MOVIN' ON

a short time after my eighth birthday Momma said that we were leaving Third Street. At the time, I didn't comprehend why it was just Momma and me. I don't recall questioning the move. In fact, I remember thinking of it as an adventure even though I didn't understand why it was just the two of us. There we were, going to our new home on East 12th Street, between Second and Third Avenues.

Our new digs turned out to be an old three-story brownstone, which had an American basement on the street level and, of all things, a front garden with one remaining huge tree (the other one was hit by lightning a few years back, we were told). This area was enclosed by a wrought iron fence and a latched garden gate. We heard that this was the only garden of its kind left in Manhattan. To the rear, at the entrance to the American basement, a wrought iron gate led to the doorway. This little alcove was directly under the stoop with its chipped stone steps. Two big glass doors at the top of the stoop opened into a vestibule and staircase leading to upper floors. In the rear of the vestibule, stairs led down to our apartment. On the first floor, a rickety wooden balcony spanned the front of two huge windows. This set up was no stranger to me. Only the street was different.

So, there we were. Our first night and we had no electricity. Con Edison hadn't turned on the juice. This handicap deprived my mother of the opportunity to prepare one of her scrumptious meals. There was no alternative but to send me to the old-fashioned grocery-deli across the street. The store was adjacent to an old stable and alleyway—remains of a time gone by. It fascinated me . . . a look at the past.

I introduced myself to the man behind the counter who gave me a friendly greeting, "Pleased ta meetcha." It was amazing what a dollar could buy. I completed my purchases and started for home, but not before I had another peek into the alleyway.

Momma had lighted some candles and we sat in the middle of the large front room on unpacked boxes. Dining by candlelight was romantic—even with my mother. It was such fun! She was in a good mood in spite of the inconvenience. I went to sleep anticipating the excitement of the next day when I would browse through the building and check out the street.

In the morning, with eagerness, I started my explorations investigating every nook and cranny. The musty smell of age conjured up visions and romantic notions in my head of what might have transpired when this place was young. Momma explained that the large bathroom on the middle floor was for the use of the roomers, as she called them.

Momma was a landlady! A dubious honor in those days. It meant hard work and a struggle to survive. She cleaned the entire building, changed linens on all beds, washed bathrooms, sinks, floors and made sure that coal heat kept the building warm and the water hot. To accomplish these chores, she rose at dawn to stoke the furnace and complete the tedious rounds that filled her day. She was a strong woman, indeed, made of that European stock that crossed half the world to get to this "Golden Land".

I tried to help as much as I could but was constantly reminded that my job was to go to school and get a good education to prepare myself for a proper place in the business world. Good heavens! I was obsessed with becoming an actor, however, I bit my tongue and nodded in agreement, feeling sure that when the right time came, Momma would fall in line. After all, there was so much time in which to do things. So much time? How wrong can you get?

Twelfth Street was one of the best in the neighborhood, populated by a diversity of economic and ethnic groups. Doctors, lawyers, Judge Aurelio (a popular, well-known adjudicator), a mix of blue collars, and the elderly who inhabited the Home for the Aged, across the street from us and closer to Second Avenue. These old citizens would sit out in front of the building, chatting with each other or with any passersby who would stop to exchange a pleasantry or two. Respect for elders was second nature to us.

It was such a great street—like a hometown where everyone knew his neighbors. The candy stores on the corners . . . the little grocery down the block . . . the apartment houses and private residences . . . and just west of our house, the factory that stretched to Third Avenue, where the "el" (elevated trains) rode by, on schedule, every day.

Occasionally, we had a little scandal, but life was good on that street.

*   *   *

Life went on simply and ascetically. I wonder sometimes how we lived through those days without the luxuries we now take for granted. The income derived from the rented rooms was minimal, even then. The average weekly rate was about $3.00 and, for an extra dollar, Momma would prepare breakfast for some of the tenants. She would pick and choose who she thought was worthy of this service, the dollar charge notwithstanding.

THE CAST OF CHARACTERS: The Roomers

My mother's favorite was Mr. Byrnes who rented one of the big front rooms on the first floor. He was a special human being, always proper in dress and well-mannered. I fondly recall hours spent listening to stories of his early years, of family memories of President Lincoln, and of his own service in World War I. We became fast friends. He taught me how to type on the old Remington typewriter which he had used as an enlistment clerk during the War. I was thrilled with the new skill I had developed.

What a strange pair we made: I, at the beginning of life's journey; he, near the end of his.

It was a wonderful day when Mother gave her permission for Mr. Byrnes to take me to the elite Westminster Dog Show at Madison Square Garden. A cab whisked us uptown. Gazing out the window at fleeting street scenes, I sat on the edge of the leather seat, anxiously anticipating what was to come. Finally, we arrived.

I had never been to the Garden. The size of it . . . the throngs of people . . . it was awesome. And, those precious canines with their best feet forward, strutting before the judges . . . they were all so beautiful and well behaved. I was deliciously happy to be there. Who else but the wealthy could afford such a pastime? I remarked that it must cost more to groom and feed these fabulous dogs than we could afford to spend upon ourselves. My comment amused Mr. Byrnes. He laughed heartily and patted me on the head.

Obviously, he was acquainted with some dog owners; after all, he did attend the show every year. How fabulous was this: rubbing elbows with the wealthy. In a sense, it did pay off for me. When we returned to the *real world* that evening, Mr. Byrnes asked Momma if she would adopt a Boston bull terrier puppy, the offspring of two blue ribbon winners. Its ear was inadvertently bitten off at birth by its mother, so the poor, little puppy was of no value in terms of show dogs. After an exclamation of sympathy, Momma consented to the adoption and soon "Chickie" was an addition to our family for many years to come.

I loved old man Byrnes for his gentleness and kindness. He was like family and Momma enjoyed making his breakfast. As he descended the back stairs to our apartment, he would herald his arrival by singing the old Negro spiritual, *"Old Black Joe"*. He loved that song and we loved the way he sang it in his quavering, tremulous voice.

He roomed with us for several years but, alas, his departure remained a mystery. One day he advised us that he was taking up residence somewhere else . . . something about a relative arranging it. We wondered about the sudden appearance of this relative. Regretfully, we never saw Mr. Byrnes again. I shall always remember that elegant gentleman, my mentor, and the touch of class he brought into our lives. Obviously, he had known a better life but valued friendship and simplicity more. Perhaps he had fallen on hard times. I can't help feeling that his first floor room represented a freedom and independence he had relinquished with reluctance when he said his Goodbyes. It left a void in our lives for a long time.

There were others who left their mark. Slight of build, brown-haired Mr. Walter Bray was a total enigma, at first. Gradually, we learned that he was a vet of WWI and a casualty of gas warfare. Before his service, he had been an editor for a Chicago newspaper. A man with a college degree, now another tragedy—a member of that lost segment of society who had served and suffered. I was fond of him even though he drank and smoked incessantly. He had a great sense of humor which I appreciated, maybe because he always laughed at my antics. His voice was grating, but his manner, gentle.

He drank so excessively, that Momma asked him to move out. Many are the times he wanted to return but there were no empties; however, he usually kept in touch. One day, I realized that we hadn't heard from Walter in weeks. It must have been Providence that I suddenly thought of him. Momma knew where he lived, so she sent me to check on him. His landlady informed, sadly, that he was found dead in his room, apparently the victim of the gas burner whose pilot light had gone out while he slept. Ironic. He was in the Bellevue Hospital Morgue but no one had come forward to claim him. His burial was scheduled for Potters' Field (a pauper's graveyard). For his sake, for his service to our country, I could not tolerate this indignity to him. At the morgue, I informed them that he was not to be moved, that as a veteran, he was entitled to a soldier's burial.

Looking back, I am amazed at the initiative I took . . . all the calls I made . . . all the people I had to see . . . but, Mr. Walter Bray was interred in a veterans' cemetery, after all.

I believe he knew.

Mr. Dave Raphaelson had a room with bath on the second floor. He was an avid photographer so he converted his bathroom into a darkroom whenever he had pictures to develop. It was fun watching or participating as he explained the fascinating process. The various pictures he took of me at different stages of my life are precious mementos.

We didn't know too much about him except that he had a son in Hollywood, California, who was an up and coming movie director/producer and that Dave might move out there someday. He was always pleasant, neat and dapper and good company. Every year, he went to sunny places on vacation and returned with an enviable suntan. Then, one winter, upon his return from Miami, Florida, he suffered a heart attack and expired before help arrived. A sorrowful experience and an image difficult to erase from my memory.

Stark reality was no stranger in our house.

The German contingent was comprised of Mr. Ernst Koch, a tall, Lurchlike figure; Mr. Charlie Unholt, small of build but solid; and red-headed Mr. Albert Miller, tall, young and handsome. They spent most of their spare time sitting on the stoop or in the backyard, speaking in their Mother Tongue, discussing the politics of the day. These men were always dressed in suits and hats, whether working or not. I learned German just listening to them. At the time, I didn't comprehend the insinuation of calling President Roosevelt President *Roosenfeld*. There was lots of talk about Germany, then in the throes of change. I don't think we were worried enough.

Everyone voiced opinions freely. There were no hard feelings. However, if someone didn't complete the chore Momma had assigned him, then he would hear about it from her in the clear, stentorian tones of a drill sergeant. If the job was done, then the reward was a home cooked meal. A treat.

These men took odd jobs with caterers or in restaurant kitchens and often brought home leftovers. Mr. Koch, especially, would proudly open a package, picking up the pieces of meat in his hands to show Momma. "Ya, Missus, this is goot." She would express her thanks, but, of course, she wouldn't touch the food with a ten foot pole.

Our dog, not particularly concerned, ate well.

Mr. Harry Kelly, another war vet and a fine Irishman, was a loner who tried to solve his hurts and problems by drinking a lot and smoking a lot. Yet, he had a gentle side and a sense of humor. Most of the tenants did. Harry kept to himself except for his daily repast in Momma's kitchen where he sat at the big oak table, near the windows facing the yard, sometimes expounding on news of the day, or just sitting quietly, staring at the outdoors.

Momma liked his quiet demeanor hence he was privy to her catering. His favorite dish was mashed potatoes and hamburgers which he chopped up and mixed together. I tried it and have been addicted to this 'specialty' ever since. When I had Shepherd's Pie in England years later, it reminded me of Harry Kelly's mish-mash.

Scottie was an amiable, bald, moon-faced Scotsman of sturdy build who rented a room for long stretches of time, disappearing and reappearing intermittently. We assumed he was off looking for employment out-of-town when he wasn't around. One day, we were sure we had seen the last of him when he left and didn't return for over a year. Suddenly, there he was at the front door. "Hello, Missus"—all smiles, and with a remarkable story: He had made his own private pilgrimage to the desert to commune with God and there he found the answer he was seeking. "Judaism is the true religion, so I converted", he told us. The whole story seemed strange.

After the shock wore off, my mother remarked that she was glad he finally found his answer but "I could have told you that and you wouldn't have had to travel so far".

Scottie stayed for a while and then vanished into the ether, never to be heard from again.

Wherever you are, Scottie, beam me up!

Henry Bogen is someone I remember fondly as a soft-spoken, frail little man who kept to himself a lot—smoking and having a drink or two, but always smiling at circumstance. When he babysat my son Jeff years later, I would fix him a sandwich and coffee and he would read or listen to the radio. Smoking or drinking were no-no's.

He roomed on 12th Street for many years and then, like so many others, faded from the scene.

I am deeply moved when I think of those days. These people were a special breed. They had a sense of independence and, although they drowned their sorrows at times, they knew they had to make a living, no matter how menial the work. Their pride did not allow them to ask for Government Relief, as though their souls would not longer be their own. I respected that.

*   *   *

The Family Guest List

Sometimes I think about the family friends that regularly visited us. Each one had a certain day, although occasionally one would overlap the other, especially when a big pinochle game was scheduled for high stakes (5 and 10 cents).

Mr. Spellman was of medium stature, always pleasant, always smiling. He was a furniture finisher and a regular hand at the big weekly game.

Mr. Fischer, a little man with nice features and a mustache and van dyke beard, was a button salesman. In Europe, he had been a rabbi. He was a close friend and didn't need a special day, so he would stop by as often as his customer stops permitted. If Momma was busy and couldn't sit down for a game or two, I would sit with him, listening to his Bible stories and stories about Jesus as a learned Jew and leader. I enjoyed the logic of his presentations.

Estelle Novitsky, Momma's girlfriend from her young days in Poland, came to visit as often as she liked and usually stayed for mother's superb cuisine. When the food got the best of her digestive tract, Estelle would blame the dog . . . but, we knew who really did it.

Mary Smith visited on Friday nights, after work. Sometimes, she brought us a box of Barricini candy from the original store in Brooklyn where she worked. Mary's daughter, Jeanette was a sweet, little girl whom I befriended and took under my wing. She still refers to me as her big sister.

Annie Lerner would visit on Thursdays. She was a soft spoken, classy, elderly lady. Momma always said that her life was a big secret. We knew she resided in an apartment hotel on Madison Avenue but she never extended an invitation to visit, except on one occasion when she invited me to visit her and "we will have lunch together". I always believed that the invitation was given out of a feeling of obligation. Whenever she came to see us, she always had correspondence that needed taking care of, and I was anointed as her secretary. My mother accepted the lunch invitation on my behalf.

Annie and I met in front of her hotel, as planned. I don't remember where we had lunch but I have a vague recollection of seeing her apartment. Maybe my imagination is playing tricks on me. Do I really recall a small, old fashioned bedroom/living room and kitchenette studio apartment that was dark in broad daylight because of the heavy drapes drawn across the windows.

When I gave Momma a full account of the day, she seemed introspective for a few minutes. "She must be so lonely in that place by herself." Momma who had so little felt sorry for Annie. When I expressed that to her, she laughed and said, "But, look at what I have, you and Morris, and so many friends. I'm a lucky woman." I loved Momma.

Mr. Harry Levine and his wife, Frieda Goodman were close friends—Harry more so than Frieda. He was a furrier; she, a dressmaker. Frieda must have been top notch because she made all of Molly Picon's costumes. Molly was one of the luminaries of the Yiddish stage, her male counterpart being Menasha Skulnick, both of whom went on to stardom on the American stage and Hollywood films. Frieda was the source of my "freebees" to the Yiddish theater on Second Avenue.

Harry was a sweet, chubby, jovial man who would bring me little fur muffs and scarves which he made from left over pieces of fur at his place of business. Later, he and Morris became partners when they leased buildings on 13th Street between 8th and 9th Avenues. Unfortunately, it turned out to be more trouble than it was worth. They put in a lot of time and hard work for naught. Overwhelming violations were heaped upon the property and eventually it was forfeited. Never buy a pig in a poke.

My mother's brothers and nephews often dropped in, unannounced, and stayed for a good meal. Momma didn't mind. She was always prepared like the Marines. There was always enough to go around. The chief priority was food in our no frills household.

Her cooking ritual began about 7 a.m. every morning: pots in position on the stove and fresh vegetables at the ready. Within a short time, the most wonderful fragrances of good, old fashioned European cooking filled the air.

Chef Esther tolerated no *ersatz* or canned ingredients in her kitchen. She made only one exception—for me—canned fruit salad when fresh fruit was not available.

Such was life in our house. In between listening to the wisdom of the old, I would relax on the divan with my movie magazines and dream of Hollywood. Of course, there was no goofing off until my homework was done—strictly regimented and supervised—then I could daydream all I wanted.

Growing up in a rooming house in the 1930's and 1940's was a unique way of life, totally different from what my friends experienced. In our house, almost everyone who entered through our portals became an integral part of our existence. Life was like a stage upon which a constant stream of events transpired—a parade of humanity with all its diversities—bringing with it a daily dose of pathos and laughter. I couldn't imagine life could be otherwise.

Yes, they were lean years but rich in the human experience. This may sound strange, but with all its monetary shortcomings and lack of fancy trappings, life was good because its main ingredients were love and hope.

Momma always said, "Every day brings a new promise".

CHAPTER 6

SEATS OF LEARNING

*F*rom ages eight to thirteen, I attended Beha Jr. High School on East 12th Street between First Avenue and Avenue A. It was an all-girls school and I like to remember it as a "finishing" school for the common people. In addition to academic subjects, we were taught art and music appreciation. Classes were taken to the auditorium on certain days to listen to beautiful classical pieces and excerpts from operas. Back in the classroom, our memory skills were tested. Who could forget *Claire de Lune, Barcarole, the William Tell Overture, Swan Lake, Carmen* or *Pagliacci*?

We learned to speak French, how to be good citizens, the art of good manners, and proper behavior in various circumstances. It is sad that today such instruction is not part of the curricula.

It was at Beha that I became fascinated with the intricacies of the English language and developed a passion for words. My teacher advised us to open the dictionary every day, select a word at random, observe its spelling and meaning, and then with our eyes closed spell the word, repeat its meaning, and use it in a sentence. I did this exercise every day for many years. When I taught school, I offered the same advice to my students. They, too, found it helpful.

My appreciation for the beauty of the French language was enhanced by the interesting and stimulating presentation by my teacher, Ms. Constance L. Schaefer. Her personal stories of life in France charmed the class, and I promised myself that I would go to Paris someday.

Momma never had trouble getting me off to school. I loved school. The difficulty lay in getting ready in the early mornings of winter. They were the toughest. The house was still cold. The heat didn't start coming up until 7 a.m. In the interim, I had to sponge-bathe at the big sink in the kitchen while my underwear warmed up on the radiator. I shivered as I dried off and quickly donned my heated under things. For a few minutes, I would plant my "tush" on the warm radiator, explaining to Momma, "I'm warming up my bones."

She would laugh, warning me, "Better get off before they are well done."

Dressing accomplished, the morning ritual followed of checking books, notebooks, pencil case and outer clothing. It was like boot camp at dawn. Finally, breakfast, and off I went.

One morning, on the first day of a new term (4th), my friends and I walked the usual route, down 12th, across Second Avenue, then to First Avenue where we waited for a signal from the policeman to cross. I was my usual talkative, animated self. Suddenly, I was lying in the middle of the Avenue. An ambulance had hit me! Why it hit *me* remains a puzzle. I walked between two friends, smack in the middle . . . how did the darn ambulance select *me*? Of course, the same ambulance that knocked me down picked me up and delivered me to nearby Beth Israel Hospital on Second Avenue.

Fortunately, when we arrived, the hospital was able to recall a surgeon who was just leaving the building. Dr. Seff was a well-known orthopedic specialist. He examined me and then spoke with Momma (who had arrived in a state of panic), advising that he could not be certain of the outcome, that he might have to amputate my leg. Well, I am ever grateful that he was able to set my compound fractured leg. He wrapped a cast around it and so it was for the rest of the school term.

My mother and Morris took excellent care of their patient. They asked for lessons to be sent home, via a classmate, so I could keep up with what was going on. The only gifts I was allowed to receive from family and friends were BOOKS, nothing else . . . no games, no candy . . . nothing but books. Momma supplied the candy and ice cream appropriately.

Morris saw to it that I spent time in the fresh air and sunlight. He would carry me outside and seat me in a large, upholstered chair and surround me with pillows and a comforter. Immeasurable care and love. Happy ending. I managed to get back to school, on crutches, for the last couple of weeks of the term, took all the exams and was promoted to 5th grade. Imagine the joy at home.

My days at Beha continued but not without incident. I did well, but my zany sense of humor was not always appreciated. My cute antics occasionally got me in trouble. Picture Momma's reaction to a request by the principal that she come to see him. After that, I got serious *real quick*, applying myself well enough to make all the rapid advance classes from 7th through 9th, which meant I gained a year and entered Washington Irving High School as a sophomore.

Except for the ambulance incident, the years at Beha Jr. High were some of the happiest of my life.

*   *   *

Washington Irving High School, at one time one of the few all-girls schools in Manhattan, is located on Irving Place between 16th and 17th Streets. It is significant in the history of education for women in New York City, not only offering courses in vocational and technical trades but also an academic curriculum. The school is directly across from the residence that Washington Irving is said to have maintained. In 1935, a bust of this illustrious author was placed in front of the school.

I arrived in 1936. Continuing my education in an all-girls school was just fine with me. (Consider the trauma later, when at sixteen, I was a freshman at *co-ed* New York University.) At Washington Irving I enjoyed a full and rewarding education. One day, in particular, will always stand out in my mind. There was an electricity, an excitement, that permeated the entire building. Teachers, principal, everyone was bustling about in anticipation of a visit by a famous guest who would address the student body during an assembly. Unfortunately, if assembly was not on your schedule that day, you were out of luck.

When I found out who the speaker was to be, I went beserk. I didn't have assembly that period. Literally in tears, I finally convinced my teacher to allow me to go, "even if I have to stand in the wings." I would have hanged from the flats, if necessary. The honored guest was my favorite person in the whole world.

Holding my breath, I positioned myself in the wings as closely as possible to the stage. At last, Mr. Zabriskie, our principal, introduced the icon. I silently shared his pride and could hardly wait to hear that soft, sweet voice and the words it would impart.

Tall, regal, conservative in dress, hair groomed in that all too familiar style, there she stood, smiling and demure. I could barely contain my fervor and desire to run on stage to embrace her. I listened as she spoke candidly of the problems facing young people, offering sound advice on being good citizens and making sensible decisions on coping in society. Her poise and self-confidence were befitting a woman of her stature. How I admired and respected her!

That superb woman was Eleanor Roosevelt.

I enjoyed the years in high school. There were times when my giggling still got me in trouble. Luckily, my teachers excused my "silliness" most of the time because I was much younger than my peers. The years went by quickly and, in 1936, I received my diploma.

My parents had applied to New York University on my behalf. At first, I was accepted as non-matriculating because I needed some extra credits. During my freshman year, I attended Washington Irving at night for credits in Commercial arithmetic and courtroom stenography. This accomplished, I was a full fledged matriculating sophomore in 1940, in the School of Commerce, Accounts and Finance (today, the Stern School of Business), on Washington Square and Fourth Street.

My time was taken up with classes, studies and student activities, except for the hours worked in the Student Work Projects office. Money earned helped pay for my books and lunches. Damages paid from the ambulance incident ($2800) took care of tuition, at first; then it became a question of putting aside money for the balance of the time until graduation. No easy task for the family.

I did take classes during two summer sessions so that I could move up my graduation to June 1942, when most of my friends were graduating. Bedecked in the customary cap and gown, sitting in the hot sun on benches at the uptown campus, the graduates were addressed by Gov. Thomas Dewey. Remembering that always makes me laugh. The dear Governor's speech was less than inspiring and several of us resorted to playing cards to wile the time away. Nobody noticed.

My parents were so proud. That made me happy. When we returned home, Morris said he was taking me out to lunch to celebrate. Momma opted to stay at home. They rarely both left the premises. Business is business.

We went to a quaint, little neighborhood restaurant and enjoyed simple fare as we chatted about the past and future. When we finished eating, I automatically reached into my purse for a cigarette, but quickly withdrew my hand, realizing I had never smoked in front of Morris before. He was aware of what had happened and, for the first time, he nodded in tacit approval. One of the few rules he had insisted upon was that I didn't smoke in front of him.

I reached a new plateau.

CHAPTER 7

LOST AND FOUND

J didn't know too much about Morris other than he had served honorably in World War I. Wounded in action, he received the Purple Heart and ribbon. Momma told me that when Morris came to America a young boy of seventeen, he had volunteered for service in the Army and served in battle as a machine gunner. Sometimes, when we sat around chatting, Morris talked about General Pershing and the battles in Europe, especially Chateau Thierry in Alsace Lorraine, France, where such a great toll was taken.

He described how the men, Howitzer machine guns in hand, advanced from fox hole to fox hole and how they fell. The enormous fatalities left a deep impression upon me. It brought me to tears. Morris spoke softly of his comrades and how fortunate he was to have survived. At one point, he did inject a bit of humor to make me laugh. "Do you know what they called baked beans? . . . conversation tablets!"

Life sometimes opens a door when we least expect it. Morris had a cousin in the bottled wine business downtown near Houston Street He would occasionally drop by. One day, he arrived in a state of excitement. A friend told him about an ad in the newspaper . . . someone named Joe was looking for Morris . . . there was a phone number to call. It was incredible. Morris had lost touch with his brother Joe after they left Europe. Could this be . . . ?

After a couple of phone calls, a meeting was arranged at our house. Indeed it was his brother Joe. He had immigrated to Canada where he met his bride in Montreal. I sat enthralled as Uncle Joe told of their pioneering days in Minitonas, Manitoba, a vast, sparsely settled Canadian territory—bush country and vastly overgrown. There, he opened a general store, the only one for miles around, but not until he had cleared the land. No easy task. He also built a lovely, little house where he and Aunt Rae and their two sons live comfortably, years of hard work notwithstanding.

Uncle Joe brought us gifts of Prince Albert china cups and saucers of the most beautiful colors and patterns, with gold or silver trim. I was curious as to why there were barely two alike. He explained: It is a Canadian custom that when company came for tea, each person had his or her own cup and saucer, used exclusively on each visit. I found it odd but quaint.

I asked him how he spent his leisure time besides having company for tea.

"Once a week, I go 'curling'."

We laughed at the name even before he finished explaining what it was. It sounded like something between bowling and shuffle board.

"Not really," he explained, "it is a game that requires extreme concentration and judgment. Far more difficult than the games you mentioned". (I would better understand this years later when I had the opportunity to watch curling.)

Morris and Joe had so much to tell each other. Every evening, while enjoying Momma's cooking, they exchanged stories. Their cousin who was influential in bringing about this wonderful reunion was welcomed at many repasts. At the time, I was working uptown for the government and left early a.m. for work. Uncle Joe was an early riser with a morning ritual. He would have his coffee with a generous splash of Myers Black Rum . . . a habit of many years, he explained.

"Necessary to get the circulation going, Uncle," I quipped. He agreed.

One morning before I left for work he insisted I have a cup of coffee the way he liked it. Needless to say, I'm glad I wasn't driving; however, it was one of the most relaxing days I've had. I told Momma it was a great way to start the day, but she had other ideas.

For the few weeks Uncle stayed with us, our mundane existence took on a new rhythm. We walked the neighborhood, telling him all about Second Avenue, pointing out important places, showing him First Avenue's market places and the variety of Italian dishes and pizzas for sale, on display on the sidewalks in front of the eateries.

He really got a kick out of the Lower East Side: Essex, Houston, Suffolk, Delancey, Orchard and Rivington Streets where the sidewalks throbbed with bargain seekers and merchants with pushcarts; where merchandise hung from old store fronts and was piled high in boxes on sidewalks. Uncle Joe couldn't get over the melee, the crowds, the gigantic heaps of merchandise. Auto traffic was almost non-existent; people browsed the streets at will.

By contrast, when we went to Greenwich Village, he was impressed by the upscale residences and their inhabitants. I explained that people in this area were mostly in the Arts: writers, actors, musicians, playwrights. We walked over to Little Italy, a popular section in the Village. He loved the colorful restaurants.

Chinatown is always fascinating and to my uncle it was like walking into a different country. The restaurants, the shops, the vendors in the streets made it one of the most colorful ethnic enclaves in the City.

Seeing Broadway was a must. One evening, we took Uncle Joe to the Roxy Theater. He marveled at the size of "such a movie house". Afterwards, we did a walking tour of the Great White Way, pointing out famous hotels, restaurants and night clubs. A swing down Fifth Avenue with its elegant window displays and then a walk in Central Park added to his amazement. He couldn't get over the stream of humanity and the vitality that was the essence of New York. I was so proud of my Manhattan.

Too soon, it was time for Uncle to return to Canada. We expressed the hope that we would see each other again. Perhaps we could visit him . . . a nice thought.

Aunt Rae did come for a brief visit and so did her son Gerry, several years later. I was able to spend time with him, showing him the sights and going to the theater to see LA PLUME DE MA TANTE, an enjoyable French romp. We even had a delicious corned beef sandwich at the famous Carnegie deli on Broadway. Gerry loved New York and years later came back to study medicine at New York University's Medical Center.

Sadly, we never did visit Uncle Joe and his family. We corresponded for years; that was all. Life is a series of entrances and exits. People enter our lives; some stay briefly, some longer. The visit with Uncle Joe remains one of my fondest memories, not only because it brought happiness to dear Morris, but it allowed me the pleasure of spending time with a fine, loving man. Whatever coincidence of fate brought Uncle Joe into our lives, I am grateful for it.

The Prince Albert cups and saucers are nestled safely on display in a special place in my breakfront. I look at them often and am reminded of days that were so sweet, so simple, so free of fear.

CHAPTER 8

GOOD OLD RADIO DAYS

*O*ur cathedral style radio stood in a corner of the kitchen. Its cabinet had a unique design with a dial bezel on a grill cloth face, the space above it showing the stations. The bezel was for low/high volume and on/off. This marvelous wooden creation was our entertainment center.

I came home from school everyday just in time to listen to Momma's favorite soaps: PORTIA FACES LIFE and THE O'NEILLs. I was permitted to listen to an hour's worth while I relaxed with a glass of milk and scrumptious, homemade sour cream cookies. Then I was relegated to my little desk in the front room where homework awaited.

If time allowed, before dinner, I played stickball or "aggies" in the street with my friends. I had quite a collection of marbles and enjoyed trading them. We played in the gutter and, strangely enough, never picked up any germs. Makes you wonder.

Dinner together every evening was the rule. We dined on wonderful culinary delights made from "scratch". No prepared, frozen, or canned stuff in Momma's kitchen. No way. Unpleasant subjects or complaints were a no-no at the table. "Not good for the digestion," Momma warned. But, when we finished eating, well, that was a different story.

Dishes were cleared and washed in time for Gabriel Heater and the news, a nightly ritual. Who could forget his signature sign-off: "And that's the way the world spins. Good night."

There were many programs we enjoyed. THE INNER SANCTUM was a favorite. Mystery and intrigue filled our kitchen with the creaking of that door and the ominous voice that asked, "Who knows what evil lurks within the hearts of men? The Shadow knows."

We found the magic of romance in SEVENTH HEAVEN and even though it left us teary eyed at times, it was a beautiful love story.

President Roosevelt's FIRESIDE CHATS kept us glued to the set. His voice and delivery mesmerized me. I diligently recorded all his commentaries in shorthand. He was handsome, charming and astute and was elected to the Presidency for four terms . . . proof of America's devotion. The nation wept when he died during his fourth term, in 1945. I was devastated when I heard the news on the radio.

Many happy hours were spent listening to personalities such as George Burns and Gracie Allen; Jimmy "Schnozzola" Durante; Edgar Bergen and Charlie McCarthy; Jack Benny (the hilarious tightwad) and his man, Rochester; banjo-eyed Eddie Cantor; and the classic comedy of Fannie Brice's Baby Snooks.

Boy wonder Orson Welles made his mark on radio and world-wide with his explosive, shocking WAR OF THE WORLDS, Halloween night, 1938. The broadcast was done as an on-the-spot news report. An excited reporter announced that a space ship had landed in New Jersey. People, panicking, were out on the streets and running toward highways. Residents were desperate to get out of the lowlands where, reportedly, the space ship had touched down and Martians were crossing the fields.

The program scared the wits out of thousands of listeners. Police were busy that night. Of course, those of us who tuned in early enough to hear Welles' disclaimer, "The following is not true . . ." remained calm. We enjoyed a good laugh but the scare it created had repercussions for a long time, providing inspiration for books and film.

The genius of Orson Welles gave us many memorable stage and movie productions, particularly CITIZEN KANE, in 1941, which is considered to be the best motion picture ever made.

Momma had her morning programs to which she would tune in just before I was leaving for school. I can't remember who sang it or what program it was, but every morning (when I was in fifth grade) as I finished breakfast, I would hear the same song: "He floats through the air with the greatest of ease, the daring young man on the flying trapeze . . .". I loved to join in, with gusto. My mother didn't find this the most pleasant way for her day to start. With exaggerated histrionics, she covered her ears and wailed, "It's too early in the morning! The neighbors will think I am killing you!" or, "You'll choke on your food if you sing while you eat!" Apparently, her remarks were unsolicited testimonials to the timbre of my voice.

Looking back, I'm not sure why it was so important for me to vocalize every morning. Perhaps I did it to make my mother laugh, or did I have a crush on that nebulous, acrobatic wonder . . . probably, a combination of the two.

> "His movements were graceful,
> All the girls he doth please,
> And my love he has taken away.
> Whoa-o-o-o, he floats . . . "

How I loved that "Whoa-o-o-o!" What visions those words conjured up in my romantic, imaginative mind: An Adonis, no less, of compact muscle and mass, like Superman or the Green Hornet, graceful, with broad shoulders and tapering torso; an appealing face with piercing, flashing cornflower blue eyes; Roman nose; sensual mouth, firm jaw—and, all this framed by a luxurious mane of midnight black that would have made Samson jealous.

Momma jolted me out of my reverie by announcing, "Time for school."

I gathered up my books, obediently, and bestowed the usual kisses. Just as I exited, I would add my mellifluous voice with one last, long "Whoa-o-o-o".

Mother always muttered, "Crazy girl", but I knew she had a smile on her face.

For years, she insisted that I was probably fantasizing the morning I was run over by that ambulance.

CHAPTER 9

THE 12ᵗʰ STREET TOWN HALL

*N*eighborhood grocery stores are endangered species, almost extinct. Tucked away in the corner of my memory are the images and fragrances of such a place and the warm exchanges of neighbors who stopped in to shop and enjoy a little conversation. If I happened to be there, I was sure to be greeted with:

"How are you, sweetheart? How's Momma? How's Papa?"

"Such a good girl shopping for her family."

"My, my, you are growing up so fast. What class are you in now?"

I would answer and the reaction would always be, "I can't believe it; you were just . . ." (whatever it was they thought they remembered) followed by a little pinch on the cheek. I loved the attention. I loved being with people.

The grocery store had a creaking, wooden plank floor and a large counter which stood at the left of the entrance. Shelves piled high with cans and jars of fruit, vegetables, jellies and condiments lined the walls. Light bulbs in sockets suspended by electric cords hung unadorned from the old tin ceiling, illuminating a variety of goods neatly and simply displayed.

The work counter was my favorite. Covered by a huge slab of marble, it was the setting for luscious breads. The wonderful fragrance of freshly ground coffee and those enormous, savory loaves—pumpernickel, seeded rye, corn, and Russian health bread—is still fresh in my mind. I can almost taste the crispy crusts crumbling in my mouth. The grocer would custom-cut these loaves and then weigh each order in the deep, old-fashioned scale suspended by chains from the ceiling. Nearby were tubs of butter and cream cheese, blocks of American, Farmer, Swiss and other varieties of cheese; cold cuts and delicious enhancers were stored in a refrigerated case.

Large baskets on the floor held loose potatoes and onions, sold by the pound. Occasionally, tomatoes and heads of lettuce were on display . . . good in a pinch; however, we usually bought our fruit and vegetables in the produce markets a couple of blocks away on First Avenue and Tenth Street.

The old grocery provided a social platform for residents who rarely ventured out of the immediate area. President Roosevelt was a favorite topic. Everyone loved him. He could do no wrong. After all, hadn't he resuscitated the economy by creating some far-reaching legislation? Hadn't he established new government agencies and re-opened the doors of the banks? Now, lots of jobs were available through various works projects. Life improved.

"Goodbye breadlines."

"Such a wonderful man . . . and his wife Eleanor . . . ah, such a treasure."

These were typical comments clearly expressing the sentiments of the neighborhood.

The overseer of this gastronomical emporium was a jovial, rotund little man. When there were no customers in the store, he sat outside the door, greeting familiar passersby. Inside, when serving a shopper, he became an encyclopedic wealth of information on everything from personal observations to statistics on the state of the economy. The store buzzed with activity. Much verbal energy was expended as he wielded his carving knife.

I loved to do errands there. Mingling with my elders made me feel grown up. Most of the time, my contribution to the conversation was nothing more than an occasional nod or a knowing smile. It felt good. This place was my chamber of commerce where I networked and gleaned tidbits of gossip that I eagerly confided when I got home.

It's sad to see the demise of the neighborhood grocery. Even though the supermarkets have their benefits, they are cold and calculating enterprises. No one cares about what's happening on your street. Just once, as I pull up to a cashier with my wagon, I wish I could hear, "How are the kids? How are things?"

I guess the mechanical, "Have a good day" is better than nothing.

CHAPTER 10

THE MOVIES IN MY LIFE

*W*hat a wonderful neighborhood Second Avenue was with all its little shops, the friendly storekeepers, and, especially the movie houses where I left reality out on the sidewalk and immersed myself for hours in a beautiful dream world. Sometimes, I cried; sometimes, I laughed. The hero always walked off "into the sunset" with his love because love always conquered all.

I believe it was that faith in the power of love that sustained many of us idealistically and emotionally during the Depression Years. We filled our hearts with hopes and dreams. The silver screen, as it was then called, allowed us to live vicariously. It was an escape hatch from bleak reality.

The movies became a vital part of my life at an early age. From the moment I stepped into a movie house, I knew I wanted to be an actor. Thanks to Momma for getting me hooked in my single digit years. By the time I was eight, I was a discerning and vocal critic and could do scenes from any movie I saw. Ask me about any film: the cast, director, producer . . . I had all the answers at my fingertips.

There are so many memories of Friday afternoons when Momma, with zealous dedication, escorted me to the Loew's Commodore on Second Avenue and Sixth Street and deposited me into a seat where I remained under the watchful eye of the lady usher. While I marveled at the saga unfolding before my eyes, she was close by, ever alert to my needs until Momma returned.

As we walked home, I was always animated and anxious to recount the whole movie . . . a habit that remained with me through the years. I loved assuming the persona of whomever was the star of the film, and by the time we arrived home, I was "in character".

I recall I did a mean Edward G. Robinson. However, I could be a lovely, tragic, ill-fated Elissa Landi. Who remembers her now? How about funny Marie Dressler who was one of the best loved actresses of the day; or, Wallace Beery who looked like a roughneck but was an actor of great sensitivity and range; or, Lionel Barrymore, brother of handsome John (the first Barrymore to win an Oscar).

So many long ago names: Warner Baxter, Mary Pickford, George Arliss (*The Great Disraeli*, an Oscar winner); Norma Shearer; Janet Gaynor (the first Oscar winner); gentle-voiced Charles Farrell; Helen Hayes (first lady of the theater); Katherine Hepburn (four-time Oscar winner); Charles Laughton; Paul Muni (Oscar for *The Story of Louis Pasteur*) . . . that handsome devil, Clark Gable wooed the lovely Claudette Colbert in *It Happened One Night* and they both won Oscars; Frederick March won an Oscar for *Dr. Jekyll and Mr. Hyde* and another for *The Best Years of our Lives*. A big favorite, two-fisted Victor McLaglen won an Oscar for *The Informer*; Bette Davis won for *Jezebel* and *Mr. Skeffington*; Joan Crawford, for *Mildred Pierce*. These wonderful actors were all luminaries of the 1930's and remained so for many decades to come.

Let's not forget that rascal Jimmy Cagney or the inscrutable face of Charlie Chan, played by Warner Oland and later by Sidney Toler; or the oh, so clever *Thin Man,* William Powell and his lovely screen wife, Myrna Loy; a salute to all the cowboys like Tom Mix, Gene Autry, Randolph Scott, John Wayne; kudos to the not always suffering heroines: the Gish sisters, Mary Pickford, Luise Rainer, Greta Garbo and Marion Davies; a special sigh for Douglas Fairbanks, Sr. as the swash-buckling, adventurous *Zorro*! and one, as well, for Douglas, Jr. who so reminded me of his father, sporting a dapper mustache and wielding a saber with panache.

Living vicariously, I forgot that times were hard. Mesmerized, I enjoyed, I suffered, I endured. I laughed myself sick at the antics of the multi-faceted, creative ability of Charlie Chaplin, dead pan Buster Keaton, serious and suited Harold Lloyd, the zany Marx Brothers, Ritz Brothers, Laurel and Hardy, Abbott and Costello. "Who's on first?" . . . all of them.

I must mention, in a class by himself, the incredibly handsome and talented Tyrone Power because I was madly in love with him. Many years down the line, I did have the pleasure of meeting him when he was appearing on stage with Katherine Cornell in *The Dark is Light Enough* (1958). That was a special time in my life.

It's amazing that film did not depend on raunchy language, overly-exposed bodies or violence of astronomical proportions. The human experience was what mattered. Nothing can replace those old black and whites. I wish they'd stop colorizing them. It takes away from the charm.

Those were enjoyable days when I sat in the dark and dreamed and laughed and cried.

I still do.

CHAPTER 11

THE JEWISH RIALTO

Second Avenue was known as the Jewish Rialto because of the numerous Yiddish theaters that flourished in the 1920s to the 1940s. The Public Theater, the Yiddish Art Theater, the Jewish Folks Theater, the Orpheum, and such, comprised a cultural giant rivaled in importance only by a vital Jewish press. Many Christian intellectuals, Lincoln Steffins and Norman and Hutchns Hapgood among them, were devotees of the Yiddish theater. They were fluent enough in German to understand the dialogue spoken by the actors. There were many others, as well, who attended, not only because they believed the productions were livelier and more interesting than Broadway but because of the passionate response of audiences. These were not bashful observers and often loudly expressed their emotions.

As much as I love Broadway, the Jewish Rialto holds a special place in my heart. I enjoyed watching fascinating versions of Shakespeare, Chekhov, O'Neill, Ibsen and the original works of Jewish playwrights—serious, comedic and musical. Those musicals were something else, filled with haunting love songs and clever, funny lyrics.

Performers were held in high regard. They held court—with the panache of the most famous Broadway actors in Sardi's—in the Café Royale, on the southeast corner of Second Avenue and East 12th Street. The Café consisted of a large room with glass storefront windows. The outside seating area was enclosed by box hedges. Admirers would stand out on the sidewalk to peek across at their favorites who often waited at the Café for casting calls. If you listened closely, you could hear writers, actors and intellectuals debating the merits of a book or play. Producers often showed up in person or telephoned looking for a particular performer.

Living just up the street afforded me the opportunity to linger near the Café, always hoping to catch a glimpse of the prestigious Adlers or musical stars like Yetta Zwerling or Aaron Lebedoff—or, perhaps the great impresario, Maurice Schwartz or Anna Tomashefsky or funny lady Molly Picon/funny man Menasha Skulnick. One of the greats to emerge and distinguish himself as a stage and film star was Paul Muni, who honed his talent on the Second Avenue Rialto.

When these stars weren't on stage or in the cafes and restaurants, they strolled the Avenue, mingling and acknowledging kudos from their fans. The Avenue was always lit up at night; people were friendly; crowds presented no fear. What a wonderful place it was! Life was warm and fuzzy. Ever so often a wave of nostalgia envelopes me and I recapture the sweet innocence of that time . . . and, how much and how often we laughed.

After all the years, a particular experience still brings a smile. Maurice Schwartz was holding auditions for a new show. A casting call was out for young girls, pre-teen to early teens. I was so excited. "Momma, you just got to let me go. This could be my big chance." I dressed carefully (with my limited wardrobe, how else?), brushed my long, blonde hair to a shine and applied a little lipstick, with nervous fingers. Destiny awaited.

Breathlessly, I ran down the street and around the corner to the huge catering/dance hall on Second Avenue where auditions were being held. Mr. Schwartz was seated at a piano next to which several girls stood in single file. I took my place on line, immediately sensing an advantage because of my height. *Being taller should give me an edge. Long hair, long legs, talent . . . I will captivate him.* Finally, my turn came. He asked me several mundane questions—name, age, schooling, what was I interested in—and studied me intently for what seemed an eternity.

Okay, what great part did he have in mind for me?

At last, he spoke. "Very nice, young lady. I'll tell you what I'd like you to do."

Yes, yes. What? Read from Shakespeare? Ibsen? Anything. I can do it.

"I would like you to begin as a dancer in the chorus line."

Chorus line! Didn't he recognize my potential as a great dramatic actor?

Taking a deep breath, I exploded, "I'm an actor, not a dancer!" And, in a most dramatic huff, I exited. I can only imagine how my haughtiness impressed him. Fool that I was . . . I messed up an opportunity to intern with one of the most famous producers/directors of the day. It wouldn't be the first time.

With tears in my eyes, I told Momma my tale of woe. She tried to console me. Finally, she resorted to her usual solution at trying times—the tea kettle.

I thought I detected a smile playing about her lips. *How could she possibly understand how shattered I felt.* I kept quiet. Hot tea and her delicious cookies, plus a kiss on the forehead, assuaged my frustration temporarily.

*   *   *

Second Avenue and some of its side streets were full of special places, many of them historic. On Second and Third Streets were two ancient cemeteries: the New York Marble Cemetery, established in 1830, between Second Avenue and the Bowery; and, the New York City Marble Cemetery, between First and Second Avenues. Several blocks up Second Avenue was Moscowitz and Lupowitz, the famous Roumanian-Jewish restaurant that played host to many Broadway luminaries who enjoyed late night suppers, serenaded by gypsy violins.

Hy Anzel, whose father was one of the partners, was a close friend when we were young, aspiring actors. We often made "rounds" together and went backstage on occasion where we met people of the theater. Hy's big ambition was to be an actor, nothing else. He would spend every penny of his allowance for acting lessons from a famous coach whose studio was across the street from The New School on West 12th Street. Hy always stopped at our house before a session. It is a pleasure now to see him in film, occasionally, and often on television in *Law and Order*.

Two other popular restaurants in the neighborhood were Ratner's and Rappaport's. Their vegetarian dishes were ingenious concoctions camouflaged to look and taste like meat. Huge piles of assorted rolls were always on the tables and *kasha varnishkes* (buckwheat groats with bowties) was always a favorite side dish. The menu offered a huge selection of goodies. This was down to earth, serious eating—a delicious memory.

Growing up, the Ottendorfer Branch Library at 135 Second Avenue was an important place for me. Religiously, I visited every week, library card in hand, and enjoyed the diversity of books available. My favorite, OLD YELLER, was the story of a dog—of course. I spent many happy hours there and felt right at home with the librarian, who called me by my first name. Momma was content that I spent a lot of time reading. Knowledge was so important, she'd always say. Although not educated, her thirst for learning always amazed me. She was one smart Momma.

(The library was erected through the charitable contribution of Mrs. Anna Ottendorfer and was a free library to the public even before there was a

New York Library system. Eventually, it became part of it. I am ever grateful to Mrs. Ottendorfer.)

A place I didn't patronize but one that always interested me was McSorley's Old Ale House at 15 East 7th Street, one of the last of the old-fashioned saloons, whose sign reads, Established 1854. This quaint watering hole—its floors covered with sawdust, a potbellied stove in the middle of the room, old décor and ambience—still exists (last time I checked). I did get to visit it once when I was grownup—a unique and charming place.

Not too far away was the Hebrew Actors' Union, a book and music store, and the First Ukrainian Assembly of God. Talk about diversity!

One of the most favorite places of mine and my friends was Auster's candy store and ice cream parlor on Second Avenue and Sixth Street. That's where the egg cream was born. Almost on a daily basis, afternoons or evening, depending on the time of year, we gathered at the counter for our egg cream fix. Auster's also served as a social mecca. In the back was a large room filled with booths where we could sit and talk for hours while enjoying some delectable ice cream creations. We played the juke box and even danced a little. Growing up was fun. We were happy with what we had.

As I said, Second Avenue was home to many historic places. At the juncture of East Tenth Street, Stuyvesant Street and Second Avenue, stands St. Mark's-in-the-Bouwerie, built on the site of the chapel originally erected by Peter Stuyvesant. Lots of history there. I passed that church every day. It always intrigued me. One day, I decided to venture inside.

I had visited local churches with friends, but from the moment I stepped through those portals, I instantly experienced a different sensation—a transition in time. There wasn't a soul in the place yet I could *see* the early Dutch congregation sitting sedately on the rows of wooden benches, psalm books open in their laps. As I stood in the center aisle, an organ suddenly began to play. Startled, I almost dashed out into the street. No matter how soft organ music sounds at times, the first few notes always seem to blast like wake-up music. Hesitantly, I glanced up at the balcony. Encouraged by the organist's friendly smile, I ventured further down the aisle until I came to the pew reserved for "Stuyvesant", right up front where I expected it to be. I ran my hand along the back of the sturdy oak bench, walled in by a waist high partition, as were all the pews reserved for special members.

Filled with emotion, I spent another few minutes imbued with the historic implications of the place which transcended any personal religious beliefs.

Years later, it struck me as ironic that Governor Stuyvesant's church stood in the midst of a highly populated Jewish area when, as history tells it, the governor was opposed to allowing the immigration of Jews to what was then, New Amsterdam.

He could never have foreseen a Jewish Rialto.

CHAPTER 12

EAST SIDE OASIS

$\mathcal{T}$he East Side and Lower East Side was home to a unique institution: the "Settlement House". These settlement houses were originally established late 19th Century to aid jobless and homeless immigrants. They set the scene for social work programs that enabled newcomers to assimilate. As time went on, they became learning and social centers, especially for youngsters. That's where I came in.

Community centers such as Christodora House, the Grand Street Settlement, the University Settlement House, the Educational Alliance and the Henry Street Settlement Playhouse, famous for its actors' group and productions, were popular youth centers. And, there was Stuyvesant Neighborhood House on East Eighth Street, between First and Second Avenue, where I spent many happy hours. These historic centers were all within a radius of a few miles from where I lived, but Stuyvesant was the closest.

Settlement houses attracted wealthy sponsors and educated patrons who were interested in social reform. University students and graduates participated, especially at the University Settlement. The experience of mingling with the working classes proved valuable and productive in influencing desirable social changes. At Stuyvesant House, we had several college students who served as club counselors and chaperons at social activities.

I was about ten years old when my friends and I joined. I had to lie about my age because my friends were a year or two older, and I wanted to be in their intermediate group. When my untruth came to light a couple of years later, it created quite a brouhaha. Ms. Banning, our benefactor, wanted to expel me immediately. She did not bend to pressure easily. Intervention from our club counselor, friends, and my tearful pleading miraculously saved the day.

Lydia Banning, a Park Avenue socialite, made Stuyvesant House her life's work. Her dedication and contribution embodied everything that was tasteful and refined, laced with a strong sense of discipline. She created an oasis for young teens to find fun and pleasure together, in the purest sense of camaraderie and friendship.

Images flood my mind: her private quarters on the top floor where no one dared enter without an invitation. This was the "Ivory Tower". Decisions were born there behind closed doors. I had the distinction of spending time there when I served as her secretary at board meetings. This honor was heaped upon me when Ms. Banning discovered my secretarial talents. A cozy fireplace, luxurious couches and chairs, fine accountrement—oh, I loved being there. For me, from the ridiculous to the sublime.

The programs initiated by Ms. Banning enabled us to participate in activities we could never have afforded, such as, classes in square dancing or interpretive dance. I loved expressing emotion through leaps and strange body movements. Actually, I had no idea what I was doing, but it appealed to my theatrical sense. Other great fun was had during sessions on the social amenities, preparing a luncheon, setting the table, proper service of each course and, best of all, making French candy.

I recall one afternoon when Ms. Banning invited some wealthy Park Avenue patrons to a luncheon catered by her "disciples". Tables were set, restaurant style, with fine linen, dinnerware and silver accessories. We girls were even dressed for the occasion in the proper attire of French maids. All the courses were prepared by us, even the dessert . . . truffles.

The knot in the pit of my stomach disappeared when I saw Ms. Banning smile with pride in our performance. I, however, promised myself that I would never work as a waitress. Too stressful! But, my table would always be properly set.

The calendar at Stuyvesant was full of scheduled events. Besides the socials, there were square dances for which we dressed the part. I braided my long hair and tried to look as much as possible like Li'l Abner's girlfried, Daisy Mae. My "pigtails" got a lot of attention. The "sheriff" kept putting me in jail and every time someone posted bail, I had to kiss my rescuer . . . but *never* under Ms. Banning's watchful eye.

Gym nights were exciting. Our basketball team played teams from other local neighborhood houses. We girls would lend our vocal talents, cheering the boys on, as the score went up—or down. Aside from the odor of perspiration that permeated the gym, it was good, clean fun with hardly a need for a four-letter expletive . . . except, maybe, for an occasional "damn" now and then. Heavens!

My club was called the Kroy-Wen's—that's New York backwards. Weren't we the clever ones? Meetings were held once a week and we enjoyed the opportunity for just "girl talk". Other evenings were taken up with special classes or events. Friday nights we had casual dance socials filled with chatter, laughter, innocent teasing and lot of dancing—hour and hours of dancing. How we enjoyed!

We felt a deep loyalty and love for each other. As children of the Depression, we didn't concern ourselves with the mercenary. Character meant much in a time of so little and we were blessed with the ability to cope and overcome.

Sunday afternoon dances were always eagerly anticipated as special. We were expected to look our best, "dressed up". A few volunteer college students chaperoned us. One summer (in my teens), a handsome William and Mary student came to Stuy to serve as a club counselor and chaperon. I don't know how it happened, but Jim and I were having the last dance together to the same song, every Sunday. Those were the days when we had crushes.

The words are still fresh in my mind (and so is his name, Jim Lucy). "Goodnight, my love, the tired old moon is descending . . . good night, my love, my moment with you now is ending . . ." He would walk me home after the dance—short lived—when Momma became aware of my escort, she nipped it in the bud immediately. I often wonder what happened to him after he returned to William and Mary. I hope life was good to him.

My friends and I spent many happy hours at Stuy and when we reached the age limit, we regretfully moved on. A traumatic transition for most of us.

The boys formed a branch of Club Rockne (named after Knute Rockne), rented an American basement on East Seventh Street, between First and Second Avenues, and became what was then known as a "cellar club" It soon became a popular meeting place for socializing and dancing. People came from all the boroughs of New York to our Friday night socials where we danced to the music of Benny Goodman, Harry James, Jimmy Dorsey, Tommy Dorsey, Glenn Miller and other big bands of the era. We even performed skits which drew attention from the local newspapers. I say "we" because I was the only female (actor that I was) allowed to participate. The boys were talented and innovative so we were able to do "take off's" on popular movies. One skit I will never forget. NINOTCHKA. During one scene, my leading man decided not to come in on cue. There I was, brushing my hair in front of my dressing table, waiting for his entrance. No show. I kept ad libbing, slowly becoming desperate. Finally, he appeared and I could detect the remnants of a smile, no doubt left over from the good laugh they had on me offstage. That's show biz!

Club Rockne enjoyed a good reputation—no drugs or other nonsense—just dancing to good music, a little flirting and romancing and lots of clean fun.

Ms. Lydia Banning had imbued in us proper values that translated into our grown up lives. Through the years, we have held reunions, creating more fond memories. Even though we are a "little long in the tooth", when the band plays a familiar tune, we are young again.

Viva the good days of yore.

CHAPTER 13

LOWER EAST SIDE

*E*ven though my territory was primarily from Fourteenth Street down to Third, I often traveled on foot to the old, interesting streets of the Lower East Side: E. Houston, Rivington, Delancey, Orchard and their environs. Walking there, especially on a Sunday, was like visiting a vast, endless market place. A colorful, ethnic mix gave the area a special flavor and character. Jews from Russia and Eastern Europe, seeking a better life, created a vital sub-culture. Street vendors with pushcarts offered items at low prices. People elbowed their way through the crowds and around the carts. Sidewalk stands were crowded with a multitude of offerings: barrels filled with pickles, counters loaded with fresh fruits and vegetables, household goods, clothing . . . just about everything imaginable.

One stop on Forsyth and E.Houston was a must: Yonah Shimmel's Knish Bakery. Those knishes enjoy a world-wide reputation. I never had trouble choosing between the potato, kasha, or cheese . . . always opted for the potato knish (with sautéed onions).

Another must, even if I couldn't afford to buy anything, was a peek in at Russ and Daughters. That place was an emporium of delectable edibles—varieties of cheese, lox, herrings, pickles, olives and smoked fishes—and on a Friday afternoon or Saturday (when Moishe's Bakery was closed) you could buy fresh bagels and bialys at Russ and Daughters. In addition, it was always a pleasure to survey the candies, nuts and dried fruits. Halvah was a popular Turkish confection, made from sesame seeds, nuts and honey. On occasion, my friends and I would pool our resources to enjoy a taste or two.

One of my favorite places was Katz's delicatessen. A walk to E.Houston made a stop at Katz's mandatory. However, that stop required the cooperation of the keeper of the exchequer: Momma. I couldn't have done it without her financial support. If Morris was with me, no problem, it was an automatic stop. Grilled hot dogs, lean corned beef, french fries and a bottle of Dr. Brown's celery tonic spelled euphoria. Katz's was always churning with activity and even when I didn't have the means, I enjoyed standing outside, watching customers vying for service, then shoving and jostling their way to a table.

I've traveled many fringe areas in lots of cities, here and abroad, but none compare with the Lower East Side. The constant ethnic vitality of the area is manifested by the expansion of Chinatown, the influx of other Asians and Indians and, in other sections, the Black and Hispanic. The Jewish community which once dominated the Lower East Side remains only a segment of it, most Jews having moved on to other localities.

It would be remiss of me not to mention the Jewish press which was the most important of the cultural institutions in the neighborhood, dealing with socialist and labor concerns. They also provided an outlet for such literary writers as Sholom Aleichem and Isaac Bashevis Singer. From these early journals evolved THE FORWARD which is a newspaper I remember well. Whenever Momma could take a break from her routine, she would ask me to read some of the columns aloud. She especially loved to listen to "A Bundle of Letters", sentimental letters to—and asking advice from—the editor. Very much like the Landers sisters advice columns later on.

The Yiddish press was only rivaled in importance by the Yiddish theater.

A lot has changed on the Lower East Side, but the essence of this city within a city, a melting pot of many ethnicities, remains.

The next time I'm in New York, I'm heading for those pickle barrels!

CHAPTER 14

COTE D'AZUR

*I*n the 1930's, Coney Island was our Riviera. We had our hey-day during the summer months going to that mecca of sand and sea. My friends and I joined the endless streams of hot, sweaty people who boarded subway trains to escape the dank, oppressive heat of steamy city streets. The clarion call of a generation of urban dwellers was, "To the beaches!" Softballs, marbles, and skates were tucked away under beds and in closets. Beach bags became standard equipment for ten glorious, sun-drenched weeks. It wasn't always the sun that drenched, but we learned to adjust.

Onward we went to the subway platforms to join the exodus that swarmed onto trains carrying us to the last stop on the line. We had great times during the 45-minute ride. Lively conversation and lots of laughter. We always knew we were about three minutes from our destination when we got a whiff of the Canarsie Canal. After one more, long, winding turn of the cars came the call of the conductor: "Co-o-oney Island!" As the doors slid open, we joined the throngs pouring out and rushed up the stairs to the street.

Fascinating attractions graced the sidewalks and Boardwalk of Coney Island, especially George C. Tilyou's Steeplechase on Seventeenth Street and Luna Park on Surf Avenue. For twenty-five cents you entered a wonderland of amazing exhibits and rides. Luna Park was a city of fire at night, lighted up by thousands of electric bulbs. It was a magic place, indeed. These were theme parks long before Disneyland . . . a world of fantasy. Penny arcades, Shoot the Chutes, Guess Your Weight barkers, refreshment stands, water slides, the Thunderbolt, the Cyclone—an endless array of rides and fun activities.

There were bath houses along the Boardwalk and on the side streets. My crowd always met somewhere between Twenty-first and Twenty-third Streets.

That's where Washington Baths was located. Although Ravenhall Baths was a bigger place, we preferred the comfortable feeling at Washington Baths where, for twenty-five cents we had the use of the pool, showers, steam rooms, lockers, and music played all day. We were permitted to dance on the walkway above the pool. All of us were dance crazy. What energy we expended! Your favorite partner was almost always your latest "crush" but we rarely were exclusive.

There were times when we didn't have the price of admission, so we met on the beach in front of the Baths. We could hear the music so we danced, danced . . . on the sand. The intrigues of growing up wore a cloak of naivete—we enjoyed the innocent simplicity of friendship in a ritual observed on Sundays in our summer place.

As much as I enjoyed the time on the beach, the best part came when we made our way to the train station. There on the corner of Stillwell Avenue stood one of the most important contributions to the culinary world: NATHAN'S FAMOUS—THE ORIGINAL. Breathes there a soul who hasn't heard of NATHAN's? I can close my eyes, inhale deeply and smell the fragrance of hot dogs grilling, chow mein sandwiches, french fries—and wonderful root beer soda to wash it all down.

Not having a few extra nickels to savor these delights was torture, especially if you had to watch your friends indulging themselves. I learned to be frugal and made sure I had two or three nickels handy even though it meant not spending a sou all day. It was well worth it. Makes my mouth water, even now.

My mother was always happy to see me tanned, healthy and in good spirits. Needless to say, the sand, ocean breezes, blessed sunlight and exercise were positive influences. When I returned home, tired and sleepy, all I could think of was going to bed and falling asleep as I reminisced about the pleasures of the day. However, Momma had other ideas. She would insist, "Eat something and tell me all about your day at the beach." The tea kettle was already chirping. How could I refuse?

One day, Morris promised to take a day off (a rare happening) and we would go to Coney Island. I was ecstatic. It was rare that we indulged in any activities away from home. Making a living always dominated. Finally, the day off arrived: bleak, chilly and overcast. The radio cautioned, "Rain today, all day." I was not one to accept defeat easily. Optimistically, I predicted, "It's going to clear up. I know it."

Not wanting to disappoint me and, in spite of Momma's incantations of doom, my father packed our suits and necessities. Off we went. A litany of "You are both crazy," and "You'll get pneumonia," followed us out the door.

After what seemed an endless ride, the train pulled into the deserted Coney Island station. Undaunted, we walked through the dreary drizzle which was rapidly becoming a downpour. We hurried through the desolate streets to the Boardwalk to Twenty-first Street. At Washington Baths, the cashier couldn't believe that we were actually buying tickets. Only one brave soul sat glumly in the coffee shop on the upper level. We exchanged hopeless glances.

We made a few feeble attempts to use the pool. Finally, with lips purple, body shivering, voice stuttering, I confessed, "I'm freezing!" Morris immediately took me up to the coffee shop, ordered hot cocoa and wrapped me in large bath towels. When I normalized, I made a unilateral decision. "Let's go home." I sensed a weight had been lifted from my father's shoulders.

As we hurried past Steeplechase and Luna Park, I thought of all the things we had planned. Alas, now there would be no long walk on the Boardwalk, no running across the hot sand to the ocean, no wafting on the waves, no sun glow and no amusement park rides. Failure, disaster . . . but, wait, there was one pleasure that Mother Nature could not deprive me of—a stop at NATHAN'S. Oh, joy, the day was saved.

Dad laughed at how happy I was to settle for my NATHAN's fix. As I munched on crunchy hot dogs and fries, I said, enthusiastically, "It was worth the trip!"

Momma greeted us with an all-knowing look. The Oracle at Adelphi, who had predicated so accurately, welcomed us warmly. She knew this would be the outcome of our frivolous excursion. On the stove, the kettle steamed; on the table, glasses for tea awaited; little cubes of sugar and slices of lemon adorned side dishes, and a serving platter was filled with, what else? Homemade sour cream cookies.

Morris and I exchanged grateful glances.

With my adept talent for humor, I described our mission impossible. We all had a good laugh. The rain pelting against the windows provided a dramatic sound track for my scenario.

*   *   *

My friends and I spent many idyllic summers at Coney Island, until it was time to move on to grown-up responsibilities and commitments.

How I yearn for those halcyon days!

CHAPTER 15

LIVIN' IT UP

*T*here's something about department stores and shops that cater to
the wealthy. A hush seems to hover over all while well-groomed,
smiling sales people quietly appear and disappear. That was my impression
in the late 1930's of Wanamaker's department store on Astor Place. It was a
classy emporium. I often meandered among the tasteful displays of clothing,
jewelry, perfumes and accessories. The sales help were kind and solicitous in
spite of the fact that I obviously was not their average patron.

Perfectly groomed and elegantly dressed ladies and gentlemen sauntered
about, stopping occasionally to ask a question or look at an item, always
quietly commenting in lowered voices. It was fun rubbing elbows with the
"upper class". My mother always said, "You have a champagne taste with a
beer pocket," but never discouraged me from wanting the best. I guess she
hoped that if I saw how the other half lived, it would inspire me to marry
into wealth.

One summer, when I found out that Wanamaker's was sponsoring a
Knitting Circle, replete with free lessons and afternoon tea, I asked Momma
if I could join. It was always a question of finances. I would have to purchase
the needles and skeins of wool. My enthusiasm carried the day. Momma
would fit it into our budget.

Off I went at the appointed time. At first, bashful and ill at ease, I quickly
became the darling of the dowagers who comprised the group. A babe in
arms. They doted and fussed over me like old aunts. I basked in the glow
of their attention. When tea and scones were served, we would chat about
things in general, but, mostly, the ladies always had questions for me: My
schooling, my pastimes, my life. I was a bit reticent to tell them too much

about my circumstances but I did speak honestly about what I did enjoy and my aspirations.

I soon became adept at knit 1, purl 1 and took on the ambitious project of making a skirt for myself. Honing my skills, I graduated to cable stitches and more intricate patterns. My dexterity knew no bounds. Even a darkened movie house did not deter me. Miss Knit 1, Purl 1, Queen of the Cables, Old Grandma—these were names conferred upon me by my friends. They never understood how I could spend time at Wanamaker's with a group of elderly ladies. Could I tell them that it was an escape to a refined, luxurious atmosphere, filled with people who lived in a different world? That knitting circle provided not only pleasure but a valuable lesson in the amenities.

*   *   *

What do you do when there's no family car and there are places that pique your interest, but you can't afford a taxi? Take a bus, of course. That's what I did almost every Sunday, weather permitting, in the late 1930's.

The Fifth Avenue bus with its open top transported me to 125th Street, on the West Side, to Grant's Tomb and Riverside Drive . . . for ten cents. I always felt the same sense of excitement as I climbed the steps topside to find a seat. Traveling up Fifth Avenue was a thrill, as I gawked at gorgeous window displays in upscale stores. Finally, after some twists and turns, the bus would arrive at Riverside Drive where I disembarked.

Walking along the tree-lined streets, I enjoyed observing the inhabitants of the area. They brought a degree of elegance to the neighborhood: actors, directors, writers and wealthy scions. The uptown dwellers. I wished that someday I would be one of them. (The closest I ever got was visiting a director I later worked with Off-Broadway who was living, at the time, in a famous actor's brownstone.)

People uptown were friendly enough. I was never concerned if a man or woman sat down next to me on one of the benches that graced the Drive and chatted me up. Spontaneous conversation on the street was not uncommon. Most people were respectable, devoid of ulterior motives, and enjoyed a friendly greeting. It's great to remember it that way.

I look back fondly upon that idyllic scene: The Hudson River sparkling in the sunlight; children sight-seeing with parents, visiting Grant's Tomb; my mingling with the crowds; an air of simple enjoyment prevailing.

At home, Momma always eagerly awaited her prodigy and the story of the day.

*　*　*

Remember when our Government asked us to collect silver paper linings from candy and cigarette wrappers? No? You missed the fun. It may sound crazy, but one of my cost-free activities was walking to Madison Avenue or Park Avenue to gather up such discarded items. I walked miles, for hours, and did well.

At home, I removed all the silver linings and added them to the ball of silver I was saving. The Government advised the weight it had to be and where to turn it in. There were designated stations where I would receive a small pittance for my trouble. But, it wasn't the money (it helped). I was truly civic minded and wanted to make a difference.

I did love the walk along Park Avenue. There was never a more impressive street with its architectural beauty. Prestigious (or, at least, wealthy) people inhabited those striking, ornate buildings. And, too, on the Avenue, strolling with their expensive little "poochies", were the high maintenance, well kept, striking looking women. Of course, I wasn't aware of how "well-kept" these lovely ladies were. It was Momma who made that clear. Emphatically clear.

So much for Park Avenue. Momma took it off my route.

*　*　*

Going to Central Park was always a hoot. Lots of free fun. Eight hundred and forty-three acres bringing nature to the heart of New York City. This was the park of the people and I loved it. Still do.

During milder seasons, my friends and I brought our roller skates and enjoyed traversing the long, endless paths. We played ball on the well kept grassy expanses. Sometimes, we picnicked. In the winter, we went sledding on the hilly sections. There was always a parent or two (my dad Morris, often) who supervised, but we didn't mind. They provided the transportation and loved to join in the fun. "After all, we are just children at heart," they would assure us.

Central Park was a romantic place for anyone so inclined. It took some growing up to find that out. By that time, my clique was mainly interested in dancing and parties. The ultimate romantic situation was playing Spin the Bottle, the most popular party game of the day. A soda bottle, milk bottle, any bottle would do. When it stopped spinning, the boy and girl at whom the bottle ends were pointing were obliged to kiss. No one voiced any objection except guess who? I was such a prude. The others would taunt me into following through. Kissing boys was not one of my priorities. I preferred to play stick ball or punch ball and run relay races with them, and win. No wonder they called me tomboy.

When we were old enough to go to the Park unsupervised, the place assumed a different persona, with new potentials. We boated on the lake, walked the bridge, watched the wild life and allowed our imaginations to wander with the balmy breezes. Sometimes, we paired off, held hands and tried to act sophisticated—men and women of the world in a picture perfect romantic setting. I must admit to an occasional kiss on the cheek and holding hands. Once in a while, a young lover would carve initials on a tree. That had to be the ultimate! That day, love was forever. Ah, youth!

Later, having my usual glass of tea with Momma, I wondered if I should confess the kiss on the cheek. I hesitated because I knew she would nix future outings, with the prediction, "This monkey business will lead to no good." I've heard that song before.

Reason prevailed. I kept my mouth shut.

Life went on.

CHAPTER 16

THE GREAT WHITE WAY

𝓕or me, the most magical place in the City is the theater district, part of the Great White Way, so-called because of the brilliant illumination from the plethora of marquees. Before the spread of legitimate theater to the Village and areas uptown, the district was located between 40th and 53rd Streets, between Sixth and Eighth Avenues.

The St. James, the Ambassador, the New Amsterdam, the Majestic, the Biltmore and the Booth were some of the most famous and well-attended theaters. In high school, my English teacher, well aware of my ambitions, bought me a ticket to see Orson Welles in HEARTBREAK HOUSE, in return for which I would review the play for the class. Morris escorted me to the theater, with the promise to pick me up after the show. I have never forgotten the experience. Orson Welles portrayed a man in his eighties (Welles was in his twenties) and some of the later-to-be stars in it were Joseph Cotton, Mady Christian, and Judith Anderson, as I recall. When I got home I couldn't stop talking about it. The next day, in class, I presented a most dynamic review, much to the delight of my teacher.

I had the pleasure of seeing luminaries like Lunt and Fontanne (husband and wife team; later had a theater named after them); Helen Hayes (a theater named for her); Paul Muni, John Gielgud, Laurence Olivier, Vivien Leigh, Clive Brooks, Margaret Phillips, Yul Brynner, Anne Jeffreys, Judith Anderson, Vivian Blaine, Johnny Desmond, David Wayne; the unforgettable Maurice Evans (whose role of Malvolio in TWELFTH NIGHT I reprised Off-Broadway years later) . . . so many beautiful, talented people, then in their prime. Many thespians "on the boards" went on to stardom in film, as well.

Anytime I want to reminisce, I browse through my collection of Playbills, which goes back to the early 1940's. They bring back many wonderful memories.

Times Square, hub of the Great White Way, at 42nd Street and Broadway, was filled with the noise of trolley cars, the smell of saloons, the dazzle of billboards, neon signs and trendy nightclubs. Sightseers, hucksters, shoeshine boys, chorus girls, models (with hatboxes in hand, the sign of the professional); actors hurrying to stages; dancers, to rehearsal studios . . . I loved every bit of being a part of it as I made my way to casting offices and cold readings.

It is difficult to omit that "breaking ground" for amateurs who honed their craft and became professionals the hard way: Burlesque. Its history is a rocky one having been frowned upon as less than acceptable as a form of entertainment. By the late 1930's, it had deteriorated into bump and grind routines and uninspired comic acts. By 1939, Mayor LaGuardia closed them down, calling them "dirty". People were fearful of cultural contamination . . . think of it! I was sixteen at the time, and, as yet, had not been exposed to the "contamination".

In the Forties, there was a renaissance of Burlesque. Believe it or not, our entry into World War II gave it impetus. Variety acts and scantily clad beauties appealed to servicemen. You can't fight that.

I must admit to going to Minsky's—one time—with a couple of girlfriends. My giggling and embarrassing vocal reactions didn't sit well with the nearby (male) patrons. An usher approached me and threatened to remove me unless I promised to behave. Stifling giggles was never easy for me, but I did, with great difficulty. Nudity always embarrassed me. And, looking around at the men with newspapers over their laps . . . well. To make matters worse later on, my friends revived the story at every opportunity providing a good laugh, much to my chagrin.

Some of the most well-known Top Bananas sharpened their skills in Burlesque: Jackie Gleason, Bert Lahr, Red Skelton, Phil Silvers, Bob Hope, Milton Berle, Eddie Cantor, Smith and Dale . . . and surely everyone remembers Abbott and Costello and their famous routine, "Who's on first?", a great spoof on nicknames of baseball players.

The Minsky brothers, possibly the most famous entrepreneurs of Burlesque, summed it up: "The tease is definitely an American art": the class act of Ann Corio; the feathered fan dance of Sally Rand; the unique, sophisticated style of Gypsy Rose Lee . . . so be it.

The huge, expansive movie houses: the Capitol, Strand, Roxy, Paramount, Loew's State all featured vaudeville acts as well as films. Big star appearances created bedlam on the streets. Lines of bobby-soxers would line the sidewalks outside of theaters to see Frank Sinatra or Martin and Lewis; Harry James and his orchestra; Jimmy and Tommy Dorsey and their orchestras. One of my childhood friends, Freddy Stewart (nee Murray Lazar) had a beautiful Irish tenor voice. He appeared with Tommy Dorsey at the Paramount and it was thrilling to visit him in his dressing room. To experience the hush in the audience later when he sang "Danny Boy" was awesome.

Ah, where are the snows of yesteryear?

Radio City Music Hall was and is one of the most spectacular movie palaces anywhere. It opened on December 27, 1932, at 1270 Sixth Avenue, in New York's Rockefeller Center. Its designer, Donald Desky, opted for contemporary Art Deco design rather then the more popular Rococco. The idea for the largest indoor theater in the world was conceived by S. L. (Roxy Theater) Rothafel, one of the great showmen of the silent screen era. The precision dance team, originally named the Roxyettes, was renamed the Rockettes, after the opening of Radio City Music Hall. Many dancing girls have come and gone, but that line of spectacular hoofers carries on. I still watch them at every opportunity, especially in the yearly televised Macy's Thanksgiving Day Parade.

In 1939, the opening of GONE WITH THE WIND was like a Hollywood premiere. The streets around Radio City were pulsating with throngs of people—those attending and those who came to watch those attending. Lucky me, I was escorted by a handsome NYU football star. Hank was not only dashing and attractive but a good student, as well. We had tickets to the opening! I couldn't get over what a special night it was.

Uptown always held a fascination for me. My first recollection of going uptown, strangely enough, is of another magical day at Radio City. Morris had promised that for my Twelfth birthday he would take me there. I could hardly wait. He told Momma that I needed a new outfit for the occasion . . . no easy task in the Thirties. Cash being hard to come by, Momma agreed we could spend $3.95, "No more!" Morris protested but Momma, queen of the exchequer, had the last word.

The outfit was not exactly Harper's Bazaar. I reluctantly settled, but Morris was not happy. He consoled me: "Next time, I'll go see some of my friends in the garment center. We'll get something nice, you'll see." I looked forward to visiting the place where fashions are born. I often did later on.

The big birthday finally arrived. I awoke with a rush of anticipation. We were going to Radio City! After a hearty breakfast and a continental rendition of Happy Birthday, off we went, with Momma's admonition to be careful ringing in our ears.

We exited the subway not far from Rockefeller Center where we stopped to view the magnificent sculpture of Atlas Holding up the World. It was lovely strolling around the manicured grounds of the Center. We had time so we sat and chatted and people-watched. When it was time, we hurried across the big avenue to the theater.

For sure, this was the palace of all movie palaces. I could barely contain myself in the gorgeous lobby while Morris bought our tickets. The place was stunning. I felt like Cinderella. I had never seen anything like it. The Grand Staircase led up to the Grand Foyer where a huge 60' x 30' mural adorned the wall. I was not sophisticated enough to interpret its meaning, but I later learned it depicted man's pursuit of eternal youth. What woman doesn't know about that?

We made our way to the orchestra and settled into plush seats. Sounds of organ music permeated the air. Looking around, I spotted an enormous organ on the balcony to our left and playing it was an elegant man in a tuxedo. I was utterly impressed. How classy! Focusing on the Great Stage, I marveled at the grandeur of it all. Morris laughed at my oh's and ah's. Soon, the lights dimmed, signaling the show was about to begin . . . the stage show, that is. Imagine . . . a stage show before you get to see the movie. My enthusiasm hit a new high.

The movie was TOP HAT, starring Fred Astaire and Ginger Rogers in one of their earliest collaborations. Their first film as dancing partners was FLYING DOWN TO RIO, in 1933. They were a great team and made an unforgettable line of great films. As wonderful as Ginger was, my eyes were riveted on Fred. I fell in love. Of course, not the same love I felt for Tyrone Power—but that's another program.

Fred epitomized grace and style, combined with a superb singing technique which made him one of the most talented and popular stars of all time. He captivated audiences. Forgotten was the Depression and that things were tough. When you watched him, you knew that everything was going to be all right. Those uplifting musicals were just what the doctor ordered.

Songwriters loved Fred. He brought a personal involvement to each rendition, and his phrasing and enunciation were impeccable. Most of his songs were written by Gershwin and Berlin. Fred had the unique knack of singing in sync with the instrumental accompaniment, creating some of the finest recordings. Alas, we shall never see a talent of his stature again. He was a phenomenon. It is interesting that one of his early interviews earned him the following evaluation: "Can't sing. Can't act. Slightly balding. Can dance a little." Sure.

As I watched TOP HAT that precious day, I was barely able to keep my feet still. I danced with Fred through every sequence. Only Morris' wary eye kept me from dancing in the aisle.

Returning home, I immediately rolled up the rug in the front room. I was Fred, that is until Momma called a halt to my terpsichorean efforts. "Time to eat. Enough with the tapping, already!" As we had dinner, I described our day. As usual, my mother enjoyed laughing at my exuberance, living vicariously, as was her pleasure.

Often through the years, I find myself humming a tune or singing those lyrics as I go about my daily activities " . . . no, no, they can't take that away from me . . .".

No, no, they can't . . . not ever.

CHAPTER 17

PREDICAMENTS, PERSONALITIES AND PRESIDENTS

The early 1930's were bleak. The country was rapidly descending into the deepest depression ever. Millions of people were unemployed. Endless bread and soup lines became a familiar sight. Veterans and penniless men sold apples on street corners. Movie newsreels showed the stream of dispossessed families from cities and farmlands hitting the roads in the only possession left to them—their beat up cars and trucks; hobos rode the rails seeking jobs and shelter. President Hoover's promise of "a chicken in every pot" never materialized. In big cities, clusters of shanties (Hoovervilles) sprung up. Here in New York City, we had our share of the hungry and the homeless. It was easy to empathize with migrants suffering in inadequate campsites and traveling from state to state, exploited and struggling to survive. It was a sad time and talked about at great length in our house.

Negativism pervaded the land. We desperately needed a change at the controls. People were fearful of the failing economy. Many withdrew whatever savings they had and banks closed their doors. Pandemonium set in (March 4, 1933). My mother was concerned that the country would go bankrupt. That's when my all-time hero went into action. Fifty-one year old Franklin Delano Roosevelt took the oath of President, moved into the oval office and called for a special session of Congress. His emergency banking bill was approved in thirty-eight minutes. Banks reopened four days later. People lined up to deposit their money again and a feeling of confidence slowly returned. Momma breathed a sigh of relief. "God should only bless President Roosevelt!"

The general feeling of the nation was, finally someone cares; we are no longer alone. The New Deal that Roosevelt envisioned and implemented changed the American way of life forever. The economy started picking up.

Society columns and radio gossipers distracted us from our daily concerns. Out of the ashes, like the Phoenix, a foundering High Society now emerged as the new Café Society. Old speakeasies became chic restaurants patronized by Café Society: the Stork Club, "21", and El Morocco. In 1938, Brenda Frazier was the Glamour Girl of the Year. I recall Cobina Wright running her a close second. What a splash their coming out parties made in all the newspapers.

Alfred Gwynne Vanderbilt—young, handsome, from old money—was the Man about Town, the male counterpart of the Glamour Girl of the Year.

I was intrigued by the whole thing and kept up with all the dirt via the gossip columns. It wasn't just the old money; included were movie stars and their sycophants, all publicity crazy. "Poor Little Rich Girl" Barbara Hutton was one of the most famous darlings of Café Society. I could never understand her title. After all, she was heir to the Woolworth fortune. With age came wisdom and I realized the inference to her series of loveless marriages.

As for me, Poor Little Poor Girl, I appreciated my circumstances even though there was usually no cash around except for the necessities. Momma's rooming house kept us secure thanks to her hard work and ingenuity. I tried to help as much as possible. For a couple of summers, I worked as a receptionist for the doctor next door, answering the phone, taking messages and greeting patients. My appearance belied my young age. Those were the good old days when doctors made house calls. I gave Momma my big salary of $12, every week.

All was not doom and gloom, however. In fabulous New York City, free of charge, I could visit the Whitney Museum (then at 8-14 West 8th Street), the American Museum of Natural History and the Hayden Planetarium (across Central Park West from the park), the Rockefeller Center complex (Fifth Avenue), the Metropolitan Museum of Art (inside Central Park), Washington Square Park, Union Square Park, Central Park, and "artsy" Greenwich Village. In addition to these were all the beautiful churches and synagogues.

A visit to the Hayden Planetarium was an awesome experience. With the celestial heavens above—stars twinkling and planets whirling—I felt privy to secrets of the universe. I really didn't understand it all but it was incredible to behold. Charles Hayden had said that the Planetarium was constructed to give the public " . . . a more lively and sincere appreciation of the magnitude of the universe . . ."

Imagine my conversation with Momma that evening.

*   *   *

Before the Empire State building, one of the tallest was the Chrysler building. It towered over the midtown Manhattan skyline. Every evening at dusk, I would watch the top of it light up. A huge clock told the time. It stood like a majestic beacon of hope. Another building that intrigued me was the Flatiron building. It was structurally unique. Shaped like a flatiron, one side faced Broadway; the other, Fifth Avenue, with both sides converging at the intersection of Twenty-third Street. New Yorkers loved it because it represented boldness and sophistication, characteristics we admired.

A nickel went a long way in five-and-ten cent stores, on subways, the ferry and the telephone. For five cents, you could buy a coke or enough stamps to mail a letter (three cents) and two postcards (one cent each). Gasoline was about a dime a gallon but not too many could afford a car, even though prices were well below a thousand dollars. Those who did own cars took to the highways, a life altering experience as new horizons opened. My escapism and adventure came by way of the movies, radio, and the "funny papers".

Sundays, Mother and Morris refrained from their usual chores and we spent the day relaxing together. It was our family day. We sat at the kitchen table reading the newspaper while Momma doted over us with her usual nourishing breakfast while we read her the latest tidbits. One thing my mother couldn't understand was what benefit could possibly be derived from reading the comics. I tried to explain that they depicted a slice of life, and in many cases, some of the characters were reminiscent of people we meet everyday. Sometimes, I could provoke a laugh from her.

On some Sundays, my mother took a break from the stove. Instead, she would send me to the Hebrew National deli on Sixth Street and Second Avenue to buy our favorites: corned beef, pastrami, a side of coleslaw and pickles. That would be dinner. For a special treat, across the Avenue was Ratner's Bakery. Fifty cents bought four of the most delectable "danishes" ever. Walking home with my goodies in hand was always pleasant because I exchanged greetings with familiar passersby.

Evenings, after we ate, we gathered around the radio to listen to Jack Benny and Mary Livingstone; the Chase and Sanborn Program with Don Ameche and Dorothy Lamour; Hollywood Playhouse, one of my favorites; Walter Winchell, fast talking as he clicked a telegraph key. "Good evening Mr. and Mrs. America and all the ships at sea . . . let's go to press"; Phil Spitalny's All Girl orchestra; the Shadow; Major Bowes Amateur Hour; Al Jolson, Martha

Raye and Parkyakarkus; the Green Hornet. I never missed the Hollywood scoop programs, like Jimmy Fiddler and Walter Winchell.

Remember Little Orphan Annie's song, selling Ovaltine: "Ya hafta earn what ya get" and seals from Ovaltine jars got you free rings, badges, secret code cards and mugs. Momma was convinced that Ovaltine with a raw egg mixed into it was the answer to a healthy me. She was sneaky about the egg. I finally got wise and we'd do battle over it.

Cowboy Tom Mix warned: "Reach for the sky! Lawbreakers always lose, straight shooters always win! It pays to shoot straight!" We were straight shooters so we bought Ralston's wheat cereal. The sponsor got rich while box tops yielded prizes like pocket knives, flashlights, rings, cowboy spurs and such. My favorite cereals, however, were Rice Krispies and Corn Flakes, in spite of my admiration for Tom.

*   *   *

The Thirties had more than its share of personalities—good and bad. Hard times spawned a boom in criminal activity. J. Edgar Hoover warned, "The criminal army in America today is on the march . . . crime is today sapping the spiritual and moral strength of America." What would he say today?

Enjoying the title of No. 1 desperado was John Dillinger. The tools of his trade were a submachine gun and a pistol. Pictures of him showed a handsome, smiling man in a hat, shirt and vested suit. Quite the Dapper Dan. I found him dashing. I wasn't one bit afraid of him. A friend of his said, "Johnny's just an ordinary fellow. Of course, he goes out and holds up banks and things, but he's really just like any other fellow, aside from that." When they asked Dillinger why he robbed banks he said, "That's where the money is."

Some people said that Dillinger stole from the rich because they robbed the poor. Sounded good to me . . . a devout fan of Robin Hood. I couldn't believe that lady in red fingered him for the police.

Shoulders above the small timers were the Barkers and Bonnie and Clyde. Ma Barker believed crime should be a family affair. She and her sons alternated between attending church on Sundays and perfecting the art of crime during the week. They quickly earned the status of all time major criminals, family style.

Clyde Barrow was a sadistic killer. He killed for the sheer pleasure of it, accompanied by his girl friend, Bonnie Parker, and a series of young men. They embarked upon a murder and robbery spree in the Mid-West which eventually brought them to a bloody end. Now, they scared me.

Bruno Richard Hauptmann was the most despised criminal in the nation. He was accused of kidnapping the twenty-month old son of aviation hero, Charles Lindbergh. I was only nine years old, but I remember the outrage and sorrow when the baby was found dead. Momma shed tears. It was almost as though everyone lost a family member. The entire nation mourned. I remember, too, the satisfaction felt by all when Hauptmann was tried and executed. The defense claimed that the verdict was a leap to judgment based upon circumstantial evidence. Through ensuing years, there were many questions that lingered. One fact cannot be denied: part of the ransom money was found in his garage.

I had a hero of my own, Amelia Earhart, the famous aviatrix. Stories of her career as a pilot always stirred the adventurer in me. I admired her. She was the bravest woman on earth. When she was lost at sea in 1937, never to be seen or heard from again, I was devastated. Conflicting stories added to the mystery that remains unsolved.

As for me, I continued to find my pleasure at the cinema. It was fun; the real world wasn't.

Saturday afternoon was movie time. Four-and-a-half hours of cliff hangers, animated cartoons, Movietone News, and two full-length films. Socrates said that we go to the theater to purge our emotions. A correct philosophical observation. In the late 1930's, action comics were launched. SUPERMAN appeared on the scene and the rest is history. At first on radio, his voice was that of Bud Collyer. In the movies, George Reeves and later Christopher Reeve are best remembered in the role. SUPERMAN lifted our spirits. He was our hero and we have been looking up to him for the past seven decades. Other icons followed—heroes of the people: Flash Gordon, Green Hornet, Bat Man.

Movies transported me to other places, other times. I lived vicariously through the settling of the West, the Civil War, World War I and the romance of the dazzling musicals so beautifully and artistically choreographed through the genius of Busby Berkeley.

I became a devotee of the dance: jitterbug, lindyhop, whatever. I could spend hours on the dance floor. We had the big bands then: Harry James, Benny Goodman, the Dorsey brothers, Glenn Miller, Sammy Kaye, Artie Shaw, Count Basie, Chick Webb and Kay Kyser. The canaries (female vocalists) handily put across the top tunes with their inimitable and varied vocal styles. Liltin' Martha Tilton, Helen O'Connell, the great jazz vocalist Billie Holiday, Mildred Bailey, Marion Hutton, and the dazzling, amazing Ella Fitzgerald, to mention a few.

My friends and I had the pleasure of seeing many of these talented performers in theaters on Broadway and dancing to their music in popular dance halls, night clubs and hotels.

There may not have been a lot of money around for some of us, but the decade of the Thirties was one of the most fruitful in terms of advances, socially and economically, and the great talent that abounded. It opened the door to unlimited potential. America was on the move with great expectations for the future.

What we didn't expect was a madman named Hitler.

CHAPTER 18

JEWELS IN THE CROWN

*T*here is nothing more glorious and elegant than the old hotels that graced Manhattan, each one unique in its style. The majesty of those grand ladies of hospitality is unforgettable. At night, they glitter and sparkle like jewels crowning the hub of activity and excitement that is the City. Some of them are still here; some are gone or replaced . . . but the memories remain.

During the 1930's and 1940's, the HOTEL TAFT was in its heyday. It was the largest midtown hotel, popular for its big band music in the basement restaurant. Many an evening you could "swing and sway with Sammy Kaye", and we did. The spectacular view of Times Square from the towers of the TAFT wasn't bad either.

The ASTOR was the popular meeting place of the day. When you made a date to meet with a friend or business associate uptown, it was customary to say, "Meet me under the clock, in the lobby of the ASTOR." A perpetuated myth was that if you were alone long enough under the clock, you were bound to see someone you knew.

The ASTOR Roof featured well-known entertainers and "dancing under the stars". It was a great place to wine, dine, and dance the night away. Evergreen is the memory of Frank Sinatra crooning to the music of Tommy Dorsey's band, as I stood right in front of him, in a trancelike state. He was really slim and one of his nicknames was "the needle".

My escort introduced me to Buddy Rich, at the time, one of the most talented drummers in the business. We enjoyed a drink together and chatted for a while.

It was truly a night to remember.

The ESSEX HOUSE, across from Central Park, was a favorite. I loved the charming sidewalk café. Nothing was more pleasant than spending an evening there wining, dining, and people watching: Chic and savvy New Yorkers; wide-eyed tourists; and others who routinely went about their business. On occasion, I saw Walter Winchell crossing the lobby. He maintained an apartment at the ESSEX for many years.

On the opposite side of the Avenue, alongside the Park, there were always several hansom cabs waiting to take you for a lovely, romantic ride through the Park and its environs. The drivers were dressed accordingly (top hats, whips in hand) and horses were at the ready. Even in those days, that ride was considered expensive.

The HOTEL PIERRE, on Fifth Avenue, with its simple elegance, attracted old money and movie celebrities. Loretta Young and Adolphe Menjou made it their New York residence. I was one day away from meeting with Loretta Young, when she was unexpectedly called away and I had to settle for an apology from her secretary. Frustrating, indeed.

I never did see the inside of the PIERRE, but I often walked by. Once in a while, I spotted Adolphe strolling the Avenue, always dapper, with cane in hand, his mustache waxed to the hilt.

One of the younger hotels, built in 1931, was the beautiful Art Deco HOTEL EDISON, on 47th Street and Broadway, right in the heart of the theater district. In the 1940's, after the theater, my friends and I stopped in at the bar to enjoy a Cuba Libre, the fashionable drink of the day.

Stories of the famed Round Table literary group that met at the ALGONQUIN during the 1920's always was of interest to me. There, Dorothy Parker held court weekly with such icons as Harpo Marx, Robert Benchley and George S. Kaufman. I wish I could have been a part of that stellar gathering. A couple of decades too late, all I could do was admire the lobby's antique desks, settees and upholstered chairs which preserved the appeal and ambience of the hotel. The atmosphere was strictly Roaring Twenties—a perfect oasis for conversation, reading or writing.

Hotel hopping was a lark—an inexpensive way to wile away the time and be a part of the energy of the City. The SHERRY-NETHERLAND, across from Central Park and adjacent to the high-end Fifth Avenue shops, wasn't far from Columbus Circle, the Museum of Modern Art, and Carnegie Hall. There was always so much to see. Stopping in for a coffee at the SHERRY-NETHERLAND gave us the opportunity to casually walk around the lobby. There was a method to our madness. What we really wanted to do (and did) was ride the wood paneled elevators, driven by white-gloved attendants. They were eye-catchers. So were the expensive boutiques.

Near my alma mater, New York University, and historic Washington Square Park, was the WASHINGTON SQUARE Hotel, with its stunning façade and Art Deco architecture. I never ventured inside but I heard that its interior walls were adorned by mosaic art works. Sorry to have missed it. It was all I could do to keep up with my classes and a job in between.

Fortunately, I didn't miss a fabulous evening at the old world, classic WALDORF-ASTORIA. In the late1940's, my cousin Leon, an importer-exporter from Turkey, was visiting. One of the questions he asked was about the WALDORF. He was particularly interested in seeing it. Leon had the appearance and bearing of a diplomat, so we received red carpet treatment in the dining room. The accent didn't hurt, either. When Leon indicated that he didn't like the table, by signaling in some strange fashion that I guess maitre d's understand, we were immediately taken to a table of his choice. A trio played nearby. I didn't think we should, but Leon insisted we dance. It was really a blast. We were fawned over and treated like royalty. My theatrical talent helped me rise to the occasion. To Leon, it seemed to be second nature.

Showing him my City was such fun.

The most precious jewel in the crown was the PLAZA on Fifth Avenue and Central Park South. The mere mention of its name conjured up images of opulence and refinement . . . the ultimate in exquisite décor, amenities, and dazzling table settings for diners.

When I was growing up, I passed the PLAZA often on my extended walking tours. Sometimes, I rode the bus to the Park and walked across Fifty-ninth Street to watch the hotel's clientele arriving or departing: Royalty, business tycoons, celebrities and families with money. Once in a while, spurred on by a sense of adventure, I walked up the front steps and bravely entered that gorgeous lobby, built of marble with gilded ceilings and imported furnishings from the world over. I felt like I stepped into a palace. It's hard to forget the ornate walls covered with paintings, enclosed displays of expensive jewelry, gift shops, and the impressively huge reception desk. Magnificent chandeliers and potted palms enhanced the grandeur of it all.

Directly ahead was the famous Palm Court, one of the many fine restaurants in the hotel, where brunch, afternoon tea, cocktails, and pre- or post-theater menus were available. The Palm Court was a European-styled café where you imbibed in good food and drink, accompanied by the romantic strains of a violin or tinkling piano. All this was too rich for my pocket, but when I started dating, I had the pleasure of enjoying coffee and dessert after an evening at the theater, courtesy of my escort. How charming that was. I loved the ambience and the personal "upgrading".

The history of the PLAZA is intriguing. It opened in 1907. The first guests to sign the register were the Vanderbilts, who were awaiting the completion of their mansion in the City. F. Scott Fitzgerald and wife Zelda were permanent guests. The Whitney's, Harriman's, Gould's . . . all nightly diners. Toscanini and Caruso entertained late hours in the Oak Room. George M. Cohan wrote famous songs there. Before my time. Too bad.

The hotel was the setting for the popular children's fictional character, Eloise. There was a pink mailbox in the gift shop where children staying at the hotel could drop Eloise a line. Cute touch. I wondered if anyone ever answered them.

I never had the pleasure of staying in one of the 805 guest rooms, however, when Cousin Leon visited again with his wife, they stayed in one of those opulent suites. They were kind enough to invite me to join them for an evening. Palatial is the word. Jaw-dropping. I had never seen rooms like that: high ceilings, crystal chandeliers, carved marble fireplace, splendid furniture and furnishings. Regal, to say the least. And, the view from the window of Central Park was breathtaking. There, too, along the sidewalk were the hansom cabs waiting for their fares.

Leon always enjoyed my wide-eyed appreciation. In fact, it made him laugh.

We had dinner in the Oak Room, after a stop at the Oak Bar. The Baroque style exuded dignified richness: Sable oak walls, murals and mosaic flooring . . . dark, but stunningly expensive. As Molly Goldberg used to say, "I was beside myself!"

We had a wonderful time together and when it was time to go home, I kissed them both, saying I hoped we would see each other again soon.

I had a lot to tell Momma that night. She verbalized it all in a word, "Oy!"

*   *   *

The PLAZA was immortalized by Hollywood in movies such as PLAZA SUITE, BREAKFAST AT TIFFANY'S, and THE WAY WE WERE.

I longed to go back some day to enjoy a scrumptious, fattening pastry and a Cappuccino, served with due diligence by a solicitous, white-gloved waiter, but, alas, it was not to be. The crown jewel has gone condo. Sad, sad, so sad.

I salute the long, successful reign of a truly majestic house.

CHAPTER 19

PARADISE LOST

$\mathcal{T}$he Davenport Theater, at 138 East 27th Street, dated back to 1915 and was the most unique of the off-Broadway theaters in its ownership, financing and presentations. (Benjamin) Butler Davenport (of the influential Stamford, Conn. Davenport's) was a talented actor with a personal crusade—to establish free theater in America for everyone to enjoy: "I have dedicated my life to spreading the idea that nobody should pay for theater admissions. We have free schools, free art museums, free symphony concerts and libraries. Why not theatres?"

There was no admission charge at the Davenport, but a collection plate was passed around to help finance the theater. Mr. Davenport spent a lot of his time and money traveling, lecturing and urging government support for free theater.

The old, gas lit brownstone was home to fascinating productions from which many actors found their way to success on Broadway and in Hollywood. Actors in between parts found a home in Davenport's brownstone where they could stay and, sometimes, participate in shows. He didn't require any money from them. Most of them paid him back when they got roles on Broadway.

Handsome Butler Davenport, wrapped in a sheet, toga style, before the footlights, was a vision to behold . . . could have been brother to John Barrymore. Before every performance, he would appear on the apron of the stage and address the audience. He spoke of the magic of stage craft and the importance of the theater as a part of our culture. It was thrilling to listen to his resonant voice of reason.

When I was a teenager, I spent many magical evenings there. One of his most impressive productions was CHARLEY'S AUNT (From Brazil Where the Nuts Come From). He not only directed but played the lead, Charley. What a performance! A tour de force of sheer genius. This role, years later, was reprised by Ray Bolger, on stage, and Jack Benny, in the movie. Davenport's superb, energetic portrayal holds a special place in my memory.

One evening, after curtain, as my friends and I prepared to leave, I was approached by one of Mr. Davenport's assistants. He asked if I would "remain a few minutes to speak with Mr. Davenport" and was I interested in becoming an actress. *Did I want to breathe?* I could barely contain myself. Speech was not an option at the moment. I could only nod enthusiastically. My friends, too, were speechless, mouths agape for a moment and then all were speaking at once, urging me on.

As I walked down the aisle, Mr. Davenport signaled me to join him on stage. With the usual amenities disposed of, he got right to the point. He had a small part in mind for me in his next production, THREE SOUTHERN BELLES. All I could do was look ready, willing and able . . . barely exhaling. He continued, telling me that he needed my parents' permission. Experiencing a momentary pang of doubt, I, nevertheless, felt sure that I was on my way to the acting career for which I so desperately yearned. I floated home.

NOT! Whatever conversation he had later with my parents spelled disaster for my dreams. In a follow-up interview, he explained that he hadn't realized how young I was, that I was still in high school. In light of my parents' concerns about my education, he urged me to adhere to their wishes. "Perhaps in a year or so . . . ." Sure. He couldn't know that with Momma it would be, "Finish high school . . . go to NYU and then . . . ?" Momma had me under contract, ad infinitum.

Life moved on. Different roads taken. Several years later, I made a sentimental journey to the Davenport Theater. Tears welled up as I watched the aging actor, still in the toga, making his customary appeal to the audience . . . like Don Quixote fighting the windmills. After the show, I was surprised when, déjà vu, I was asked to come to the stage for a word with Mr. Davenport. This time, he prefaced his conversation with, "I thought you were Stella Adler sitting out there in the audience. You look just like her." Well, that was flattering in itself, but I would have preferred, "Aren't you Diane Bryan? Maybe now you can join my acting company."

I reminded him of our earlier connection; now, only a vague recollection, he admitted. We spoke for a while. He expressed his fear regarding the tenure of his theater and its survival. There was such sadness in his voice. Instinctively, I knew this was to be our last visit together. Always those other roads.

I don't know exactly when it became the Gramercy Arts Theater, but, since 1968, it has been home to the Repertorio Espanol.

The Davenport was given the title of historic landmark by the City of New York, as off-Broadway's oldest theater.

How often through the years I think of that road not taken.

Paradise lost.

*   *   *

NOTE: Benjamin Butler Davenport died in 1958, at the age of 86, in his apartment above his beloved theater, on Twenty-seventh Street. Night after night, he told his audience, "I've been tremendously rich in everything but money."

I am proud to have known and been a devotee of this dedicated theatrical genius.

CHAPTER 20

TAKE ME TO THE FAIR

a red letter year for me . . . and New York . . . was 1939. On January 8th, I turned sweet sixteen and entered NYU as a freshman; on April 30th, the New York World's Fair opened. Two exciting events, to be sure.

Of course, I wanted to go to the Fair so Momma arranged for a family friend, a gracious elderly gentleman, to escort me. Arriving at the number sixteen did not mean that I could take off for "foreign" places by myself. Queens was unexplored territory, "so far from the City". Eager to go, I voiced no objection to a chaperon.

The moment we arrived, my mouth dropped open in amazement and remained that way for most of the day. Grover Whalen, President of the Fair, called it "The World of Tomorrow". Looking around at the technological marvels and amazing gimmicks, you would have to agree. First of all, just viewing the 10,000 trees and the million planted tulips from Holland, plus the illuminated fountains, was spectacular. It was hard to believe that this incredible Fair was built on a Queens' city dump.

There were miles and miles of paved streets and footpaths and I tried to cover them all. A lost cause. I took pity on Momma's friend. However, I did enjoy indulging in the luscious Belgian waffles with ice cream, not to mention other goodies and exotic foods from foreign lands, offered by a multitude of vendors. Eating aside, the stunning gimmicks and side shows, the Zoo, the New York Cultural Pavilion, huge futuristic buildings housing the representations of over a thousand exhibitors, and a variety of impressive demonstrations—from Ford Motor Company to the Dr. Scholl's Footease—were mind boggling.

The high points in the amusement zone were the Cyclone Roller Coaster on which brave souls were strapped into little, open compartments which hurtled down and around curves, spiraled upwards, only to drop quickly down again. As those cars dropped, so did my stomach. I declined to participate in the 250' parachute jump sponsored by the Life Saver candy company. It wasn't easy watching it—exciting, yes—but scary. (Little did I dream years later, at a parachute jump in Coney Island, I would take the dare.)

It was fun to watch Elsie, the cow, being milked electronically on a merry-go-round and another exhibit called "A Thousand Times Neigh", a horse's-eye view of the automobile. At the General Motors pavilion, Futurama predicted what the 1960's would be like. How far off it all seemed! The Dance Pavilion featured Lindy Hop dancers; my favorite dance. I wished I had a dance partner with me. Momma's dear, old friend couldn't cut it.

One of my cherished memories of the day was Billy Rose's Aquacade where swimming champions Esther Williams and Johnny Weismuller, handsome specimens of grace and agility, displayed their exceptional talents in that artificial waterway built for the Aquacade. Williams was discovered there by an MGM talent scout and went on to stardom in the movies. Weissmuller already was a star from his *Tarzan, the Ape Man* movies. Watching them was quite thrilling.

The Fair was a spectacular achievement, "a magnificent spectacle of a luminous world, apparently suspended in space . . ." (from the Official Fair Guide Book). It was symbolic of the visions and dreams of people fighting to free themselves from a long struggle through hard times. For post-depression New York, it was a shot in the arm.

In July that year, Life magazine observed, " . . . and your fellow fairgoers trudge on numbed feet with dazed eyes." That about summed it up for me.

When I staggered into the kitchen that evening, the kettle was steaming on the stove, and Momma was waiting patiently for my report. Tired as I was, my enthusiasm hadn't waned as I eagerly described the wonders of the Fair. Momma was incredulous. She was sure some of the details were spawned from my fertile imagination. After I persisted—insisted—she finally shook her head in awe.

"Wunderbar! Who could ever imagine . . . ?"

"I wish you could have been with me, Momma. Maybe someday we can go?"

Momma smiled. "Maybe." I doubted it but said nothing. She rarely left home.

It was only 1939! What more could the future hold in store?

CHAPTER 21

A HORSE, A HORSE,
MY KINGDOM FOR . . .

*I*n time, my friends and I looked for new activities to fill our recreational hours. We expanded our sphere of fun. Some of the boys were now driving cars, so we could go out of town—like, Long Island for miniature golf and hot dogs at Howard Johnson's on Queens Boulevard; or, a ride upstate to Monticello for a day in the country. It was great to escape the steaming city streets in summer. When someone suggested horseback riding, the idea was greeted with enthusiasm. A new experience for most of us. Early Sunday mornings we made the trek to riding stables outside the City limits.

It was 1941 and I was a junior at New York University. Working in the National Youth Administration office after classes enabled me to pay for lunches and books. I was even able to save a few coppers; hence, I could afford a snazzy black and white checked shirt, black jodhpurs and jodhpur boots—and the riding fees.

One of the boys heard about a real Western style ranch in New Jersey. We jumped upon the idea. Going for the breakfast ride at the Triple "K" required getting up at five in the morning, to arrive at the ranch by 6:30 a.m. No problem for me, but Momma, as usual, was beside herself. "You have to be crazy! Who ever heard of getting up at five o'clock in the morning to ride a horse?"

When I answered, "Cowboys do it all the time," she gave me a look that zippered my mouth shut. I knew one more word and Momma would raise the drawbridge. Morris winked at me, suggesting that I get ready. The beep of a horn signaled the arrival of my friends. I quickly kissed Mother and Morris goodbye. "Meshugina" followed me as I raced out the door.

Two cars, filled to overflowing, waited at the curb. Adventure time! We were so excited, going to unfamiliar territory . . . to New Jersey. As the roads grew more rural, our anticipation mounted. We sang along with the radio, teased and made jokes and were just plain silly. A lovely, carefree time.

Finally, arriving at the Triple "K", we tumbled out of the vehicles to view a vista of barns, stables, and a huge farmhouse and voiced our surprise at the authenticity of the "spread". Warm, friendly hosts greeted us and explained the schedule for the day. At the stables, we were assigned horses. One of the ranch hands escorted us to the bridle path. He remained with us throughout the ride, helping to refine our "seats", instructing us how to post, canter, and gallop. When he commented that I had a good seat, I was embarrassed—until I found out he meant I sat well in the saddle. Go know!

One of our friends, Jack, did not sit so well. A heavy set guy, he had trouble co-ordinating his seat with his saddle. His large sized jodhpurs inflated and deflated as his derriere moved out of sync with his horse's canter. I couldn't help but laugh hysterically, so much so that my long, pinned up hair came undone and cascaded around my face and shoulders. Our trail escort rode up, asking if anything was wrong. All I could do was point to the "bellows" in front of me and continue to shake with laughter.

When I explained what had happened to the others riding up front, poor Jack became the recipient of wise cracks which, however, didn't alter his amiable disposition one bit. I wasn't side-saddle or naked, but my companions chose to call me Lady Godiva for the rest of the day. Score evened.

After about an hour, our guide led us back to the stables where we took leave of our faithful steeds. He then escorted us down a path to the large mess hall. We were seated on benches attached to large, wooden picnic style tables laden with fresh juices and fruit. Pots of brewed coffee and pitchers of milk were handy. The fragrance from the platters heaped with fried bacon, sausages and baked biscuits filled the air. Sizzling skillets of eggs, hashed brown potatoes and pancakes followed. Our appetites did justice to that delicious, satiating meal while our hosts hovered over us and ranch hands stood by to serve our needs.

It was a superb day. Every moment was filled with laughter and camaraderie. We hated to leave. Finally, our weary little group said Goodbye, promising to return in the near future. Why not? Everything was going according to plan. The day was young and we would be home early enough to attend the wedding of a friend of ours. We joked about changing into our fancy duds for the big event.

On the way home, the music on the radio supplied the usual backdrop while we exchanged impressions of the day. Suddenly, the music was interrupted by an announcement. We didn't catch it all at first . . . something about a Pearl Harbor . . . the Japanese. Quieting down to listen, we were struck dumb by the reporter's words. The Japanese had attacked Pearl Harbor. A terrible silence fell upon us; then we all began speaking at once . . . questioning, wondering.

Our lives were changed forever. Nothing would ever be the same after that Sunday—December 7th, 1941.

The next day, President Roosevelt announced that it was "a day that would live in infamy" and declared war on Japan and the Axis nations.

Classes went on as usual at NYU that day, and in the late morning, the entire student body heard, via loud speakers, the President's declaration. Everything came to a halt at that moment—in the classrooms, the hallways, and out on the street. Some of us were on our free period, having lunch in the juke joint across from the School of Commerce. When the speakers began blaring, we hit the street, standing there in silence, absorbing the impact of the President's words. No one, nothing moved. An eerie, solemn quiet pervaded. Then, suddenly, we were all talking at once. I heard the word enlistment mentioned. The whole scene was surrealistic.

We came of age that day. Innocence lost. Serious contemplation defined our plans. Good times melted away like paint on a clown's face in the rain.

Too soon, some of our friends bid us Goodbye—not only classmates but, more so, dear friends from my neighborhood. Down at Club Rockne, the topic of the day was enlistment. More than half a dozen enlisted right away, not waiting for draft notices. The rest soon followed. They served in all branches of the Service. Those who were sent to nearby camps, temporarily, came home on leave to march in a neighborhood parade before shipping out. I spent my senior year trying hard to complete my studies while, on a daily basis, I wrote letters, letters, letters to my G.I.'s.

I had a girlfriend-boyfriend understanding with one fellow, in particular—Henny, who was well-spoken, handsome and lots of fun. He worked during the day and attended City College at night. One of the first to enlist, he was soon eligible for officer's training in the Air Corps. I turned down his invitation to spend time with him in Chicago before he was to start Officers' Training at Chanute Field, Illinois. I yielded to Momma's firm, "No!"

because I was still in my teens and the implication of such a trip frightened me, anyway. Sad to say, I never saw Henny again. His B-19 was shot down over Kiel, Germany, during a massive bombardment of its munitions factories. His pictures and letters have a special place among my mementos.

That was one of the rare times I regretted listening to Momma.

When the War ended, some friends returned from the European and Pacific theaters of operation. Some did not. I remember them all with love.

CHAPTER 22

GREENWICH VILLAGE DAYS

*G*reenwich Village was always a special place: a hub of activity enveloped in an aura of mystery and fascination, not only for New Yorkers like me, but for visitors from all over the world. It was like an intimate little town within a teeming metropolis, loved by enthusiasts of the Arts and home to writers, actors, authors, artists and musicians.

The tree studded streets of the Village were lined with unique little shops offering a plethora of items from antiques and jewelry to clothing and house wares—all exotic and upscale. Sidewalk cafes were popular for sipping coffee or cappuccino and watching the parade go by.

On a breezy day, the delectable aroma of garlic and basil from the restaurants filled the air. Little Italy, as it was referred to, was a popular ethnic area . . . always lots of people in the streets, music playing, storekeepers calling to one another with the latest bit of humor . . . ah, things seemed so uncomplicated then.

Even as a child, I was consumed with interest in the Village. It was like a private club where you dared not venture unless you "belonged". I was confident I would penetrate that veil when I became an actor.

The gods were good. I didn't have to wait that long. Morris came home one day and told Momma about an opportunity to lease the upper floor of the corner building above Whelan's Drugstore on West 8th Street. The furnished rooms on that floor were rented to roomers, just like in our brownstone. Morris was enthused. He explained that it was right in the hub of Greenwich Village, flanked on one side by a huge intersection. Broadway, Astor Place, Sixth Avenue, Christopher and Greenwich Streets all fed into that circle.

Nearby was Washington Square Park, the campus of New York University. "It's a wonderful opportunity," he told Momma. "Let's do it."

After much discussion about arranging for loans and then negotiating with Whelan the deal was consummated—but, not before Momma met with the landlord's representative. She had to pass judgment which translated into "looking into his eyes" and playing a game of pinochle with him. Momma always asserted that she could judge a person's character that way. The gentleman passed the test.

A new door opened in our lives.

It was so exciting when we went to check out the premises. The place intrigued me. It had an aura of mystery about it. I was convinced that there were obscure nooks and crannies behind sealed doors. The rooms followed each other like box cars as the floor wound around the turns in the old structure. Morris pointed out that the glass enclosed room at the head of the stairs would make a convenient office from which he could monitor the comings and goings of tenants.

Momma always worried that he spent too much time tending to chores at both properties. Luckily, he was able to retain the housekeeper, Dora, who changed linens and cleaned the rooms. But, there was still the heat, hot water, collecting rents and doing the bookkeeping for both places. His day started at six o'clock in the morning when he carried out the barrels of ashes to the front of our house, and then went to West Eighth Street and did the same, before settling in at the office. He always managed to be home for dinner, on time. Momma was a stickler about that.

At the time, I was a freshman at New York University. It was great to be able to walk over to see Morris. I sometimes did my assignment in his office, but the best part was cruising around the neighborhood, looking into store windows, and browsing some of the shops. I rarely made a purchase but it was fun.

There was one place I couldn't resist visiting at least once. It was a famous though antiquated tearoom, up a flight of iron stairs from the sidewalk. I suppose what I recall more than the actual physical aspects of it was the ambience. Stepping inside was like going from stark reality into sepia tones of the past . . . fleeting images, as if filtered through gauze, blend in my memory: little tables and velvet upholstered chairs, metal lamps with beaded shades that tinkled every time the door opened, admitting a breeze. Through the years, on occasion, I have closed my eyes to recapture and "hear" the quiet of that tearoom. The hushed whispers and low-key conversation of patrons as serving ladies maneuvered about, their long-apron dresses swishing softly in contrast to the loud hustle-bustle outside. It was de-lovely, to quote Cole Porter.

Another memory lingers about that street. A true relic of the past was a small, cobblestone side street. Original gas lit lamps on their posts still stood like silent sentinels in front of old brownstone residences that framed the cul-de-sac. Every time I glanced into that almost hidden alleyway, my imagination conjured up images of another time: horse-drawn carriages pulling up with dashing, handsome men calling on fashionably garmented ladies, whisking them off to elegant, chandeliered restaurants and clubs where they wined, dined, and danced the night away.

I often wonder if that little side street still exists, particularly, because I remember a controversy ensued over doing away with it, several years ago, long after I left the City. Luckily, at that time, petitions and a furor came to the rescue. I was happy to hear that.

The money I earned at the University from the National Youth Administration was used for books and lunches. A few blocks down on MacDougal Street at Horn and Hardart's, I could get a hot meal of spaghetti, green peas and carrots, a roll and a drink for twenty-five cents. I did almost as well in the juke joint across from the school with a roast beef and coleslaw sandwich, french fries, and a pineapple coke. I was on a no-nonsense budget.

*　　*　　*

I miss the years at NYU and the time spent in the Village. Many afternoons, at Morris' office, I participated in lively conversations with some of the tenants. That place had its share of the strange as well as the talented—a trip in itself.

There was no finer person than Mr. Alfred Grundel, a Swedish gentleman who had the bearing and breeding of a man of letters. Apparently, he had come upon hard times but, mysteriously, appeared to have an income of sorts. I know he ran short at times because Morris financed a lunch now and then. Mr. Grundel adopted us as family. When he could afford it, he sent us flowers and Barricini candy, which he purchased at the shop across the street. In those days, Barricini was the equivalent of what Lady Godiva or Baci-Baci is today.

Mr. Grundel was also a collector of books. He often sent me home with one which made Momma happy. I still have some books and cherish them, especially the huge 1918 edition of Funk and Wagnall's dictionary—original and unabridged. The book is an amazing conglomeration and monumental study of the English language and testimony to the changes it has endured.

Of the other roomers, I remember one couple, in particular. The man was a published poet of some renown—Bernhardt, I believe, was his last name—I'm not sure. He and his wife rented a room for a while. They squandered their funds away on liquor and were usually behind in their rent. Although Morris admonished them and tried to reform them, it was of no avail. Finally, with great remorse, Morris asked them to vacate the premises. Several months later, we learned, sadly, that after a night of debauchery, a stranger they had invited to join them in their quarters murdered them . . . a pitiful ending for our poet and his lady.

Morris sponsored many free lunches for people in need. He was truly a Good Samaritan who trusted and loved people. Proof of this is in the way he lived his life, sensitive to the needs of his family, his fellow man and God's creatures. In return, everyone loved him, even the crazies in the Village. My mother and I wondered how a man so timid and reserved was able to handle the mélange of characters with whom he dealt. Experience is always the best teacher, I suppose.

*　　*　　*

While still a student at the University (1941), I was accepted as an actor member of the Greenwich Village Art Workshop, a theatrical company. The director, Liz McCormick, was a most talented lady. The Workshop was a wonderful training ground. A unique group—all female—we met and rehearsed evenings in a large loft in the Village. Liz shanghaied directors, stage hands, and make-up men to visit us and offer constructive, instructive advice for our journey to the bright lights of Broadway.

A year later, we did two off-Broadway productions: Shakespeare's TWELFTH NIGHT (I mentioned this before) and THE WOMEN in which I played the vicious Sylvia. This role was played by Roz Russell in the movie. I was flattered when a member of the audience came backstage, marched up to me and declared, "How I hated you!"

I couldn't have gotten a better compliment. Realism is the true test of any portrayal, whether on stage or in film.

CHAPTER 23

THE WOEFUL DAYS OF WAR

*M*y theatrical aspirations were put on hold. After graduation in June 1942, I went to work for the New York State Department of Labor on Ninth Avenue, in Manhattan. I became a war bride in August when I married Alexander, the father of my oldest son, Jeffrey. He was drafted into the Army and I continued to work for the Labor Department, in the legal steno pool. Soon, I was promoted to secretary of the Wages and Hour Unit which, after a directive from Washington, D.C., became the War Labor Board. Suddenly, there I was, the *first* secretary of the WLB in the United States. The unit quickly grew into a division and I was designated the Executive Secretary. For a while, I was happy to meet the rigors of this demanding job, but with the war escalating, I decided to join the Navy.

I made sure I met all the requirements of enlistment, even to correcting the teeth in my mouth, and applied for a commission in the WAVES. All went well. I was ready for the last phase of my physical. I didn't sweat it. I was healthy and strong. Patiently, I sat before the recruiting officer, awaiting my assignment to Officers' Training. Well, picture this: Taking my hand in hers, the officer said, "You aren't going to be a *WAVE*, you're going to be a *mother.*"

. I continued at the War Labor Board, supervising the typing, steno and clerical pools and handling the director's correspondence. Ever so often, Mr. Theodore Kheel would visit the WLB to meet with the director. I always sat in to take dictation. "Teddy" Kheel was impressive: young, astute and handsome—always puffing away at his pipe, deep in thought. Intuitively, I knew he was destined to make his mark in U. S. Labor relations and negotiations. The years proved me correct.

It was with much regret that I had to hand in my resignation. It was time to be home with Momma and Morris to await my baby's arrival. Our family doctor lived across the street. A comforting thought. How well I remember Dr. Ganz, black medical satchel in hand, trudging along as he made his house calls all hours of the day and night. That's what doctors did in those days. They answered the call for help at anytime, often at great expense to their own well-being. Luckily, he had only to cross the street to see me.

On 17 September 1943, I gave birth to my adorable, longhaired boy, Jeffrey. Recovering from a bit of an aftermath, I was soon strong enough to get on with it. My husband, in the interim, graduated Second Lieutenant from Officers' Candidate School in Louisiana and was shipped out to Newport News, Virginia. Like a good Army wife, I packed up and, with Jeff in hand, headed south.

Momma and Morris accompanied us to Grand Central Station. Oh, the tears that flowed as we stood there amidst the bustling crowds of servicemen, their dear ones clinging and kissing and hugging them, saying their goodbyes. My parents were too distraught to say anything. They just kept kissing Jeffrey and looking at me with such sadness, dreading the inevitable goodbye. Finally, they had no choice.

Off I went, babe in arms, to Virginia where, on a blustery night, we left the railroad car to board the ferry that would take us across Chesapeake Bay to Newport News. We were surrounded by servicemen who were most helpful. Otherwise, I can't imagine how I would have managed a baby, a valise, and a couple of shoulder bags—and still remained upright on the rocky crossing. The wind was howling; the air, freezing cold. All I could think of was, *What's a nice girl like me doing in a place like this?*

Alexander had rented a little beach house out in the boondocks. It wasn't easy for any of us. Within a short while, without warning, my husband was shipped out in a convoy and I found myself stranded, in a quandary. I had no idea what my next move should be. I decided to go to the source, the base in town. After pleading with the brass, they allowed me to speak with my husband for only a minute or so or I would "endanger the convoy". Quickly, the decision was made that Jeff and I would return to New York in our car. Luckily, one of the soldiers was going home to New Jersey and he offered to drive us to Manhattan. Was I ever thankful!

Needless to say, my parents were overjoyed when we arrived but it was a short-lived reunion. Too soon, we were on the move again. Alexander was now stationed at the Army base in the Baltimore Port of Embarkation, in Maryland. We found an apartment in Middle River and settled in—or, so I thought.

Momma's fear that the move would prove disastrous came to fruition after a few months, but for an unexpected reason. Being left alone for days on end with a little one, miles out of Baltimore proper, was not what I anticipated. The story had the usual cast of characters with the usual suspects: neglected wife and child; self-centered husband; lots of available females. Big heartache. I severed the ties by removing Mr. Wonderful from the premises . . . at great emotional cost.

I accepted a secretarial job in the real estate office just down the street. Fortunately, my neighbor and close friend Anne agreed to baby sit, so we were both able to supplement our incomes. Sixty dollars a month from Uncle Sam did not go far.

A college chum of mine and her Captain husband lived around the corner. This was a fortuitous coincidence. When I received word that the real estate office was closing, the Captain approached me with the offer of a position as a civilian attached to the Air Corps, on the base where he was the medical officer. I jumped at the opportunity. At last, a chance to serve.

At 6:30 a.m., Monday through Friday, I took the bus to the 3530th AAFBU, not far from Glenn L. Martin Aircraft, where the first B-29 was manufactured. My job was to prepare, organize and maintain supply records . . . to create a system replete with cross-reference files. When I was shown to my office and opened the desk drawers, I asked, "Where are the records and files?" The Staff Sergeant and Warrant Officer looked at each other and laughed. There was only one property turn-in slip and one quartermaster requisition in sight. My work was cut out for me.

It was a demanding job but I felt a sense of achievement as file cabinets gradually filled the room and even a safe with prioritized information to which only I and the officers had access.

Every night I was home with my little boy and we had dinner together. Weekends were special. We took rides on the bus to Baltimore where we sometimes went to the movies or took lunch with us to a local park or the beach. I recall one beach visit in particular. As we sat on our blanket enjoying the fresh air, eating our lunch, I noticed a sign nearby that read RESTRICTED AREA. When I asked a park attendant what the sign meant, he answered, "No colored, no Jews." I decided that would be up to me. My son was enjoying the God-given fresh air and sunshine. No stinking sign was going to deprive us of a pleasant afternoon.

I tried to go home on an occasional weekend, whenever I could. It was so good to be on home turf and spending time with my parents. They could hardly wait until I completed my service at the base.

After serving a little more than a year, orders came to deactivate. The Navy was taking over. Our Captain, the "Old Man", called me in to thank me for my "dedication to duty" and to inform me that St. Louis Eastern Command was sending an auditor for a final review of our records. Guess who was asked to remain and secure all files?

Finally, after weeks of hard work, it was time to say goodbye to the 3530th. Time to go home.

I never did get that service ribbon promised me. But that's not what it was all about.

CHAPTER 24

THE RETURN OF THE NATIVE

*H*ome once again in my beloved City and back to the old brownstone for a while. Momma and Morris were happy to have their grandchild to dote over. They loved Jeff dearly and looked after him when I worked for the American Red Cross (attached to their Washington office) here in Manhattan. Based upon my experience, once again I handled supply. When that assignment ended, I was asked to stay as secretary to the Director of the New York City Red Cross. The Director was a wonderful person and a gentleman. His assistant, however, chased me around the desks in hot pursuit, whenever I had to work late. Imagine, if that was happening these days!

Living at home was great, but I felt it was an imposition. We were really too cramped to be comfortable. At least, I thought so for my parents' sake. As soon as possible, I rented a room for me and Jeff in the corner apartment house on Second Avenue and 12th, on the same side of the street. We had a small bedroom/living room combo with a community kitchen in the hallway—a common set up in those days.

Luckily, Momma was just down the block, so we spent most of our time there. I had to be careful that we did not stay past ten o'clock. That's when elevator service ceased at the apartment house. A minute past ten and I had to carry my robust son up five flights to our small abode. Many are the times we left "Ga-ma" and "Bram-pa" a few minutes too late.

Pretty soon, Momma insisted we come back, crowded and all. "So what? So we'll manage!" I always tried to abide by her philosophy: "You make your bed; you sleep in it." I couldn't believe she was letting me sleep in her bed now, but I was grateful.

Luckily, many of my friends did return from service in the War. They had been through horrific times. Fatigue and trauma were evident in their attitudes. It hurt to listen to their pain. I spent as much time as I could with them. Often, they came to the house and Momma welcomed them. A sense of innocence, of hopes and dreams, was lost. It was obvious when they spoke about the future. So much had changed since they left. Now, suddenly, they were civilians without direction . . . what to do, where to find work . . . how to get over the devastation they had witnessed. That was the hardest part—getting over the wounding, the maiming, the dying of their comrades and friends.

Talking . . . lots of talking . . . was so important. Even magazines and newspapers ran articles by psychologists and sociologists urging help with readjustment problems. Thank goodness, most G.I.'s were eventually caught up in the changes they discovered: television, new gadgets, new personalities in politics and entertainment, and lots of new fads.

During the next few years, many veterans were members of the "52-20" Club—unemployed, discharged servicemen who received $20 per week for 52 weeks. Some took government loans and opened their own businesses; some opted for college educations . . . tuition and living expenses generously offered them under the G.I. Bill of Rights.

After World War II, New York wore a different face, a face changed by the influx of people from other parts of the United States, and worldwide. Servicemen who had spent time here during the War, now wanted to make New York their home—a new land of opportunity . . . of glamour, beauty and grace . . . abounding with the stuff of which dreams are made.

*   *   *

Being a single mother is not easy—ever. I know. I tried it a couple of times. Anyway, ever an optimist, I did marry again. Buddy was a Navy vet and an old friend. His parents had a linoleum store on the corner of Third Street and First Avenue, and he worked for them. I didn't think this was the right path for him, but they did. He was quite talented in things electronic. Delehanty Institute was offering courses in all aspects of that *new* industry: Television. No charge for veterans. Urging Buddy to take advantage of this opportunity fell upon deaf ears.

After the War, finding a place to live was difficult. Having no alternative, we settled into a cold water flat, shared toilet in the hall, in a dilapidated building on Third Street, between Second and First Avenues, conveniently a few doors away from the family store. The building was easily a hundred years old. Its iron staircase in front, flanked on either side by glass storefronts on the first level, led to dingy, dark hallways and more iron stairways. We were lucky to have found even that dismal, two-room back apartment. What had to suffice for our bathing needs was a large kitchen sink, which also served as the facility for washing clothes and dishes. Wasn't that a kick in the head? And, I thought Momma's brownstone was tough.

After a year or so, I became pregnant. Desperate; I didn't want to bring my baby into that awful place. It was enough that Jeff's bed barely fit into a tiny alcove under the staircase. Fortunately, Morris came to the rescue. Ever alert to an opportunity for better housing for us, he found and negotiated the purchase of an old brownstone at 130 East 17th Street, between Third Avenue and Irving Place. We were mortgaged to the hilt but happy and excited. I don't know how he managed the deal, but he did, and just in time.

My beautiful, strawberry blonde daughter Ellen-Carole was born on 20 June 1948, just a month or so before we moved in. We spent the time at my parents' house until we took occupancy. New baby furniture and teddy bears awaited my daughter's arrival and a new bedroom set and games for Jeff. It was a happy time even though we faced a tremendous amount of renovation and refurbishing.

Morris stopped by every morning with something Momma had cooked and goodies for the children. Almost every day, after Jeff came home from school, the children and I would go to Tompkins Square Park where we had good times socializing. In those days, parks were the social centers for mommies and their children. No "play dates", just simple times filled with fun, in the fresh air with friends.

I guess I was destined to live in American basements. I didn't mind. We even had a backyard. Living in brownstones is like taking a step into the past. Or, at least it was then. The building was over a century old. The massive, wooden doors at the entrance at the top of the stoop bore the coat of arms of the wealthy family who had resided there. I heard somewhere that it had been the City residence of the Morgan's. I was impressed.

The first floor had a large, front living room/bedroom and a similar one in back. Both contained a small kitchen corner across from which was a wooden platform where an ancient, footed bathtub stood, with a shower head attachment. Privacy was achieved by drawing a curtain around the metal framework above the tub. A commode was available in a water closet in the hall, which was shared by both tenants on the first floor.

The apartments were furnished with antiquated furniture, lamps and rugs and diffused an aura of long past elegance. It stirred the imagination. Beautiful marble fireplaces graced both quarters.

The rooms on the two floors above were singles. Some had sinks; some, showers, as well. All contained the basics: a bed, dresser with wash stand, chair, lamp and clothes closet. Each floor had a community bathroom. The top floor, which was referred to as half-a-story, had low ceilings and small chambers. Originally, these rooms housed the servants of the wealthy residents.

The basement was something else. Unlike Momma's, it did not store coal (we had oil heat) but it did house various items of interest like crockery, metal artifacts, pieces of furniture and a variety of framed pictures. There were also several huge paintings. I recall one, in particular. It was of a beautiful, nude brunette, lithe of body, reclining. I often wondered who she was and why the artist had painted her, only to leave her behind in that dark, dank cellar. It provided some interesting mental gymnastics.

I couldn't get over living next door to Washington Irving High School. Every once in a while, I'd go out into the back yard and listen to the sounds emanating from the windows of the school . . . sounds that brought back so many memories. How long ago was it that I was reprimanded for giggling and sent out of the classroom to control myself? . . . or could barely contain my composure when Mrs. Fischer taught typing by hitting a yardstick against the letters on a huge pictured keyboard in back of her as she, facing us, shouted out the letters . . . or struggled through basic Algebra and never would have passed if Nancy Pappas had not helped me . . . or how much I enjoyed advanced French and stenography? As I stood there daydreaming, a whole panorama of scenes unwound themselves, unraveling like a roll of celluloid film.

Living in the brownstone was not all fun and games. It had to earn us a living. How well I knew the routine! Every Friday was change of linens and general building clean up. Starting at 6 o'clock in the morning, I prepared my Friday night dinner, got Jeff off to school, made my daughter comfortable and had everything in order by the time I went upstairs to do my chores. Buddy and I cleaned the entire building and then he would go to the family store. The rest of the week, I ran the show, renting rooms, and, in general, overseeing and collecting rents.

The weary must relax so we set aside Saturdays to take the children to Central Park where they loved visiting the monkeys in the Zoo and watching the gigantic seals in their huge pond. The Park had a cafeteria where we enjoyed lunch. It was a pleasant way to spend the day in that beautiful oasis, not too far from home.

On Sundays, we were more adventurous and traveled further. One place we loved was Alley Pond Park in Queens. We packed up enough food for three meals and, at six o'clock in the morning, loaded up the car and off we went. In those years, Queens Boulevard was a long, wide road with an occasional house or business on it, as I recall. We felt like we were out in the country. By the time we got to the Park, we were ravenous, so breakfast was in order. Buddy's family usually got there earlier and reserved tables and barbeque pits for the whole bunch of us. We spent the day playing games, cooking and eating, reading, talking—whatever, and returning home, at night, totally exhausted, but feeling healthy and stress free.

Sometimes, we drove out to Jones' Beach on a Sunday, where we enjoyed the water and fresh salt air and spent the day eating and relaxing. It was a long ride but well worth it.

Life was good.

CHAPTER 25

GRAMERCY PARK TIDBITS

J had a previous acquaintance with the area. While in high school, I got the opportunity to work with a newspaper woman who lived in the elegant, Old World Gramercy Park Hotel. She inquired at the school if they could recommend a student to help edit her writing. It was quite a thrill for me when I was chosen. I vaguely recall there was a small stipend involved (twenty-five cents an hour?)—actually, not so small, at the time. I enjoyed the evenings spent in her charming apartment, sitting on the plush rug on the floor, surrounded by pages and pages of copy. She wrote about her trips to Russia and what life was really like there, under a communist regime. She used a male pseudonym so as not to blow her cover. Going to Russia in any capacity was pretty tricky then. Working with her was like being a part of her adventures; I loved it.

Little did I dream, I would be a resident of that area a decade later.

*　*　*

Back to the future. The big move to Seventeenth Street transported us into a totally different environment. It was hard to believe that life could be so different, only a few blocks and an avenue away. We lived on the fringe of what is known as Gramercy Park which ran from Eighteenth Street to Twenty-first Street, from Park Avenue South to Second Avenue. The name Gramercy derives from the Dutch "crommesie" (crooked knife), so called for a meandering brook in the area. The district was once a prosperous row house neighborhood, but eventually many were replaced by apartment houses (circa late 1920's).

Gramercy Park is a small, charming, historic place. Like so many, I believed that Washington Irving, the writer, had lived at Forty-nine Irving Place, corner of Seventeenth Street where, it was said, he wrote some of his most famous novels: *The Legend of Sleepy Hollow* and *The Sketch Book*. I later found out that his relatives refuted this but admitted that, at times, he did stay with cousins at 120 East 17th Street—an exciting fact because I lived at "130"—albeit, a century later.

Ever curious about his supposed residence, I delved into some research which resulted in interesting data. In the 1890's, its famous tenants were Elsie de Wolfe, actor, and Elizabeth Marbury, a powerful literary agent whose clients included Oscar Wilde and George Bernard Shaw. Elsie and Elizabeth were a famous lesbian pair who held popular salons in their home. Among the attendees, old money, like the Astor's, and new talent like Sara Bernhardt, plus playwrights and luminaries of the stage.

How I would have loved to attend those salons! I was born too late.

The Gramercy area was fashioned after a London style square: a park in the middle, surrounded by the houses of its inhabitants. Gramercy Park was a private park, therefore, only residents of Gramercy held keys to it. If you were a guest at the Gramercy Park Hotel, as a bonus, you were given a key to the Park for as long as your stay. The Park is a lovely green oasis, enclosed by a wrought iron fence that seems to banish the turmoil of the City. It was a place of peace and grace and beauty. New Yorkers love it even though most of them will never get inside. I consider myself one of the lucky ones.

A short while after moving to Seventeenth Street, I made a delightful friend—Dora—a well-known artist for Conde Nast publications, who lived on East Eighteenth Street and Irving Place. An official Gramercy resident, she was one of the "key privileged". Her daughter Stephanie and my son Jeff were the same age and got along famously. Dora and I spent pleasant hours together in the Park, chatting, while the children played games and my daughter Ellen snoozed in her carriage.

One day, there was a big scandal in the neighborhood: John Garfield had been found dead in one of the residences near the Park. After dining at Luchow's restaurant on Fourteenth Street, with a friend, he returned with her to her house, where he suffered a massive heart attack. The authorities were called and, of course, gossip spread quickly. (Garfield was married.) I admired John Garfield and would not dwell on the negative. We had lost a beloved and talented actor. His funeral at Riverside Chapel drew thousands of mourners (including *moi*). The crowds were reminiscent of Rudolph Valentino's funeral where throngs lined the streets, waiting to pay their respects.

Dora and I chatted quite a bit about Garfield's demise and decided that his personal business was his own. In time, the ill wind that blew through the Gramercy, died down and the incident took its place in newspaper archives.

It was that time of year and the Barnum and Bailey Circus was in town. I had never been to a circus. One afternoon, Dora surprised us with tickets for center box seats at the Old Madison Square Garden. She and I and the children were going the next day. Well, what a fabulous time it was. The children were captivated by the side-shows, high wire acts and the performing elephants, tigers and lions. Soda and cotton candy kept the adrenaline going. It was truly an enchanted time.

The Old Madison Square Garden had a second floor where Stanford White, the famous architect, had his bachelor pad. It became famous in the headlines when he was killed by a jealous husband in the Rooftop Garden supper club theater. It was said that he had a red velvet swing built in his pad for his girlfriend, Evelyn Nesbit, a Floradora girl. The murder achieved great notoriety and inspired the movies *Ragtime* and *The Girl on the Red Velvet Swing*. The story persisted through the years. I reminded Dora of it and that provoked a lively discussion.

On several occasions, I was invited up to Dora's studio apartment where I met her handsome artist husband and enjoyed their hospitality. I was surprised at the pristine décor. We sat in captains' chairs in what served as her living room. I didn't mind, in fact, I felt very bohemian . . . artsy, to be honest. I always enjoyed that milieu.

There were (and are) so many places of interest and history in Gramercy. I often took walks past the National Arts Club located in the Tilden Mansion at 15 Gramercy Park South. It is a New York landmark and National Historic landmark. The purpose of the Club is to stimulate, foster and promote interest in the arts and to educate Americans. It is famous for its tradition of inclusivity: recognizing important female artists, minority artists and is a defender of minority students' rights.

My favorite walk was to the Players' Club at 16 East 20th Street. The Club was founded by Edwin Booth, the great Edwardian actor (brother of the infamous John Wilkes). Other famous members of the Club were Mark Twain, Arthur Miller, Carol Burnett, and Margaret Hamilton. I liked to walk there because it was not unusual to see the familiar face of an actor, on occasion.

Nineteenth Street between Irving Place and Third Avenue is another block with a special reputation. In the early part of the Twentieth Century, there was a revival of the row houses, done over with stucco and tiles. Unusual artistic touches embellished them. It became known as the Block Beautiful and housed an informal colony of artists and writers, during the 1920's and 1930's, who were known to have sponsored some wild parties. Ethel Barrymore, talented sister of John and Lionel, once said, "I went there in the evening a young girl and came away in the morning an old woman." There you have it.

The Gramercy was always such a classy place. Even Hollywood paid visits. There was a famous little cellar book store on Irving Place and I was told that it had been used in films. Imagine the excitement when Hollywood took over the streets for about a week. They were shooting scenes for an upcoming Rex Harrison film and the book store was a part of it. The scene started there and progressed to my street whereon Mr. Harrison walked right past me. Just imagine *my* excitement! I was out there everyday, mugging for the cameras but, alas, I was not discovered. Drat!

Momma got a kick out of that story.

Some addresses of long ago residents:

Actor Theda Bara .... 132 E. 19th Street
Author John Steinbeck .... 38 Gramercy Park E.
Inventor Thos. Edison .... 24 Gramercy Park S.
Author Booth Tarkington .... 26 Gramercy Park S.
Author Edith Wharton .... 14 W. 23 Street
Poet/Playwright Oscar Wilde .... 47 Irving Place

In years to come, there were so many other celebrities who made Gramercy their home and still do.

I often look back and wish I had stayed, but . . . that darned door keeps opening and closing.

CHAPTER 26

THE STREET OF THE WALL

$\mathcal{T}$he wall, built as a defense for New York City, is long gone, but Wall Street lives on as one of the most internationally famous places in the world. It houses the New York Stock Exchange, a vital part and barometer of our economic lifeline. There, some of the most important business deals are executed: where promises are made—sometimes, kept; sometimes, broken. It is an exciting arena. Masses pour in at the start of the day, spilling out into cabs and subways at day's end.

Long ago, on Wall Street, there was a small eating place where you sat on a stool at a circular counter and ordered a cup of coffee, a nut bread with cream cheese sandwich, and a delectable donut, if you wished. That was Chockfull O'Nuts and I was a dedicated member of its clientele. How did that happen?

After my in-laws closed the store, it left us with a decision as to supplementing our income. My husband agreed to stay at home, manage the brownstone and look after the children. I would seek employment. Good fortune intervened and on my first interview I was hired by Clark-Robinson Corporation as their legal secretary. The manager of the office was a fellow NYU alumnus. After speaking with me, he advised that I be hired, sure that I was qualified for the position. Talk about being in the right place at the right time!

The president and vice-president of the firm were quite congenial, and the attorney to whom I was assigned was a gentleman and most cooperative. I had it made. In fact, it was the vice-president of the company that encouraged me to take insurance brokerage classes, which I did, and was one of the fifty percent that passed what was reported to be the most difficult exam ever given in the field. That I succeeded still amazes me. I counted my blessings and happily applied for my license.

The work of a legal secretary is no walk in the park, but I had experienced the grind in the New York Labor Department, so I welcomed the challenge. Involved in the mystique that was Wall Street gave me a feeling of *being*. I looked forward to my daily routine. Dressed in black, pearls at the throat, one in each ear, and white gloves—that was the "uniform" of the secretary . . . it was a sophisticated look and I loved it. Of course, my long hair was done up in a braided or butterfly bun.

As to Chockfull lunches, I did not need the entire hour for eating and, seats being at a premium, I didn't take up a seat longer than necessary. Depending on the time, I cruised the neighborhood shops and mingled with the teeming crowds out on lunch hour. Occasionally, I stopped at a pet shop off my usual route. There, destiny awaited me and a beautiful Shepherd Collie puppy. I noticed that the rest of the litter was doing all the eating while this little one was forced back into a corner by her siblings. She looked so frightened. I approached the shopkeeper, asking why this was going on. He explained that sometimes a litter will gang up on one of its own, but he did see to it that she ate.

On my visits to the pet shop, I always witnessed the same scene. I tried to perk the puppy up with kind words and pats on the head. Images of her haunted me for days. Finally, I decided if the dog was still available, she's mine. I returned during a lunch hour and made a commitment. After work, I picked up my new "baby". No subway ride that evening. I hailed a cab and arrived home about an hour later than usual. My family's concern turned to joy when I emerged with my precious bundle. It didn't take long for Princess to settle in and enjoy our love and attention, which she returned twofold.

Too soon, it was time to call a halt to my business career (for personal reasons). I gave my notice reluctantly. My lunch hours were spent at Chockfull's until the day before my departure. That final day, as a fond farewell, my employers treated me to a posh lunch at one of the upscale restaurants that catered to attorneys and other professional Wall Street denizens. As usual, I was impressed by the linen, china and crystal. I felt like Cinderella. *For sure, they would ask me to clean the office later*. With cocktail in hand, fine faire, and lively conversation I savored the moment . . . happy, yet sad.

On the walk back to the office, we passed Chockfull O'Nuts. For a moment, I peered through the window at the circular counter where I had enjoyed so many simple lunches. I mouthed a quick Goodbye and felt like I was losing a friend.

At the close of the business day, everyone lined up to hug me and wish me well. My employers gave me a striking pair of cufflinks (I loved shirts with French cuffs). I thanked everyone for the time spent with them and hurried out as tears began to well up.

Walking to the subway, I looked around, my mind recording images. Before I descended the steps to the station platform, I turned once more to glance down that hectic thoroughfare. *I'll miss you, street of the wall.*

Another door closes.

Strangely, another had opened, unexpectedly. Morris had a stroke. He was always so strong and healthy—it was such a shock. We decided that he and Momma should live with us. For several years, they occupied the apartment directly above ours. I helped as much as possible and rode the ambulance with him, on many occasions, to the Veterans' Hospital on Kingsbridge Road in the Bronx. His last stay was in Northport Veterans' Hospital on Long Island. Momma and I often took the Long Island Railroad on weekends to visit him.

On one such trip, Momma said she had to tell me something . . . that it was time. I couldn't imagine what it could be. As she unraveled the details of my birth and adoption, about which not a word had ever been spoken, I could do nothing more than listen . . . speechless. *I remembered once saying, "How can I be your daughter? We are so different!" How that must have hurt.* Taking her hand in mine, I said, "Momma, you are the only Mother I have known. You brought me up . . . gave me as much as you could . . . I'm *your* daughter, Momma." She squeezed my hand and I could see how difficult this must have been for her. We never spoke of it again.

Door locked.

CHAPTER 27

CHANGE OF VENUE

*T*he 1950's was a fast changing decade. We found new heroes while old ones came crashing down.

Martin Luther King became the brilliant, exemplary spokesman for the black civil rights movement and a young actor, James Dean, became a symbol for his generation in REBEL WITHOUT A CAUSE. General Dwight D. Eisenhower, ever popular with the people, received a record thirty-three million votes in a time of peace and was elected President of the United States in 1953. He had a winning grin and enjoyed a reputation as a home-grown moderate—open minded—but politically shrewd. What he wanted most was for the people to remember him as fair and as their friend.

J. Robert Oppenheimer, atomic scientist, fell from glory, when witch-hunting bureaucrats besmirched his character. But, there's no doubting the impact of his work in the Manhattan Project. Americans reacted to atomic power in different ways. Some, seeking adventure, rushed off to Colorado or the wilds of Canada to seek their fortune in uranium. Some dug bomb shelters or purchased the pre-fab ones. At any rate, neither fared well. Uranium seekers never became wealthy and the shelters were soon used as storage areas.

For the first time, in 1952, television brought the Republican and Democratic Conventions live to the public . . . with all their foot stomping and sign waving and screaming. The CBS commentator that covered the conventions was Walter Cronkite, one of America's foremost journalists and a favorite of televiewers.

Yes, the times they were a-changing. Hula-hoops, Marilyn Monroe and then Elvis. He made rock and roll a "religion" for teen-agers. Despite criticism about Elvis' bumps, grinds and shimmies, Elvis Presley emerged as one of the most influential entertainers of all time.

We religiously watched Milton Berle, Arthur Godfrey and, of course, everybody loved Lucille Ball and Desi Arnaz (I LOVE LUCYshow). Other popular sit-coms were THE HONEYMOONERS, MAMA, FATHER KNOWS BEST, THE PHIL SILVERS SHOW, WHAT'S MY LINE . . . to mention a few.

The cultural changes that occurred affected all of us. TV absorbed too much of our time. People weren't reading . . . or thinking . . . as much. Mass media was being devoured at a high rate and the quality of some things was questionable. However, the die-hards did demonstrate a sense of responsibility by promoting programs of cultural works in literature, plays, art and music. We were saved.

The streets on the East Side gradually filled with new inhabitants. Hell's Angels, a motorcycle club, now occupied buildings in the area, especially on Third Street. The roar of their engines violated the air. Old timers in the neighborhood were not comfortable, in fact, they were fearful of the group. Yet, there were stories of good deeds.

Seventeenth Street, too, was showing a different face. Overcrowding in the City was becoming a big problem. I witnessed people on our block (immigrants) sharing rented rooms, taking turns sleeping while others waited in the street all hours of the night. Some passed the time playing guitars and singing nostalgic songs. Nice . . . if you aren't a light sleeper. The straw that finally broke my back was the murder that was committed across the street. Earlier in the day, two men had had a disagreement about American politics as it affected Puerto Rico's independence. That evening, the man who had argued against U.S. policy, returned to finish what he had started. He knocked on the door and when it opened, he fired, killing the unfortunate fellow with whom he had disagreed earlier.

My husband and I, together with my parents, had a long talk. Especially because I was pregnant with my third child, we decided it was time to join the exodus to Long Island for that halcyon life of fresh air and flowers.

EPILOGUE

*N*ew York City has a magic that rubs off on people. It gives its inhabitants *the edge*.

I have a running love affair with the City. I love the hustle-bustle, the mad rush of people going places, honking cabs, buses, lights flashing—the stream of humanity oozing out of the multitude of huge buildings and skyscrapers—the fellowship among New Yorkers and the sense of pride.

As we drove out of the City on that last day, I looked out at the passing images and wondered how I would survive out on the Island. I sighed and consoled myself. *Not to worry. You will find your way back to the bright lights.*

I didn't want to go—to leave my first love—but I had to. Gradually, the trauma of departing from the City took second place to the excitement of a new home, a new place, and the anticipation of the birth of my baby. But, I knew Long Island wouldn't—couldn't—compare with my fabulous Manhattan.

We were leaving a week later than planned because we had received a telegram from the Government that our loving Morris had passed away, on the very day we were set to leave. That was September 1954, and dear Momma left us in June 1955, just a few months before my baby was due. We were already residing in Bethpage.

Living in a split level was a new and strange experience. The kitchen, dining room and living room were on the street level; three bedrooms and two baths, on the balcony level; a huge playroom a few steps down from the kitchen; and below that, a full cellar. It seemed so grandiose. No more American basement for me.

On 16 October 1955, Jonathan, my handsome, blue-eyed boy was born. It was a pleasure to bring him home to his own room in a new house. A funny thing happened after I brought him home from the hospital. Our dog Princess was really not privy to the goings on. She probably thought I had been away on vacation and greeted me warmly. I immediately went upstairs, put Jonathan in his crib and returned to the living room. As we sat and chatted, suddenly, there was a loud wail from the bedroom. Princess leaped so-o-o high and dashed up the steps to see what stranger had invaded our home. Not knowing what to expect, I ran up right behind her to explain. Once that was established and she implemented a "sniffing" I.D. test, Princess rarely left Jonathan's side.

Jeff and Ellen were registered in school and we settled into a routine. Jonathan lounged in his carriage, with Princess on guard duty. Buddy went to New York every day to work and check on the brownstone. I still had my insurance broker's license, so I sold insurance from the house. Life was good . . . I thought.

Within the year, my creative genes were in an uproar. I yearned for the opportunity to tread the boards again. Before long, I was participating in local group productions. Eventually, I formed my own regional theater company, THEATERAMA; was asked to participate in summer theater (in the round) productions of Town Dock Theater in Port Washington—pretty far off-Broadway, but exquisitely satisfying. Ah, those memorable years . . . but that's another book.

Not so satisfying was the turmoil that developed in my personal life. Soon, I found myself in the role of single mother, again. Because earning a living was top priority, it was back to university for me. After student teaching at JFK Jr. High School in Bethpage, I was retained as a full time English teacher (1960). It was a double blessing. I met Jack Murphy and when we retired we headed for Florida. Here in Boca Raton, I found my long delayed niche: writing. I wrote articles and opinion pieces for local papers, graduating to editorials in the Boca Raton News (picture and by-line, to boot). I moved on to becoming an author: my first novel, SOLDIER OF GOD, and my second, JOURNEYS, were both published within the last few years, and now my MEMOIR OF MANHATTAN. Not a bad third act.

Jack passed on recently . . . a great loss for me, the family, his friends and his colleagues at the Broward Teachers' Union. I'm fortunate that my children, Jack's children and grandchildren are close. They are my raison d'etre.

So, life is still good.

But, as Jackie Gleason used to say, "Look out for them swingin' doors!"